FACTS AND FICTION

FACTS AND FICTION

A book of storytelling

Michael Holroyd

BLOOMSBURY PUBLISHING
LONDON · OXFORD · NEW YORK · NEW DELHI · SYDNEY

BLOOMSBURY PUBLISHING
Bloomsbury Publishing Plc
50 Bedford Square, London, WC1B 3DP, UK

BLOOMSBURY, BLOOMSBURY PUBLISHING and the Diana logo
are trademarks of Bloomsbury Publishing Plc

First published in Great Britain 2018
Copyright © Michael Holroyd, 2018

Michael Holroyd has asserted his right under the Copyright, Designs
and Patents Act, 1988, to be identified as Author of this work

For legal purposes the Introductory Note on p. 1
constitutes an extension of this copyright page

A catalogue record for this book is available from the British Library

ISBN: HB: 978-1-4088-9735-5; EBOOK: 978-1-4088-9736-2

2 4 6 8 10 9 7 5 3 1

Typeset by Integra Software Services Pvt. Ltd.
Printed and bound in Great Britain by CPI Group (UK) Ltd, Croydon CR0 4YY

To find out more about our authors and books visit www.bloomsbury.com
and sign up for our newsletters

Contents

Introductory Note

I do not know exactly how I chose the subjects for these essays and articles over the last twenty years. It is something of a mystery – and I enjoy mysteries. One or two of them can be linked to minor characters in my biographies, and I came across others in the books of other writers. But most of them seem to have reached me accidentally. These were happy accidents and even happier when they found some magazine or newspaper that gently paid me for their publication long before they eventually elbowed themselves into this book. They appeared all over the place: in the *Charleston Souvenir Programme*, the *London Magazine*, the *Folio Society*, the *Times Literary Supplement*, the *Guardian*, the *Financial Times*, the *Telegraph*, the *Spectator*, *New Statesman* and *Slightly Foxed*. Almost all of them that appear in this volume were written during the twentieth century, but the earliest one was first published in 1979, beginning not with a birth but a death: the death of my grandfather or, as I saw it, his many deaths.

I am grateful for initial guidance from Caradoc King at United Agents and also the encouragement from the Bloomsbury team: the publishing director Michael Fishwick, Kate Quarry the copy-editor, Jasmine Horsey, the assistant editor, Francesca Sturiale in charge of production, the publicist Chloe Foster and Angelique Tran Van Sang who kept us all amiably in contact.

PART ONE

Fact and Fiction

No one asked me to be a biographer. Quite the opposite. My grandfather hoped I might set off for India and make a career at the tea plantations there. He had been presented with some shares in one of the Assam tea companies by his father. He used these shares as if they were tickets that took him on a summer holiday, which he called 'following the business'. What he really wanted was to go abroad without his family from time to time. I saw a photo of him in India once: he was smiling in a way I had never seem him smile at home. And he was encircled by rather bemused-looking planters.

Back at home he taught me the skills of making a proper cup of tea. It was not easy: how to hold the cup correctly; how to boil the water to an exact temperature – and then how to engage the small spoons of tea with water at the right moment. Then there was the difficulty of preparing the milk and adding it. Sugar was never tolerated. Writing a biography was far easier than preparing a correct cup of tea – or so it seemed to me. In the end I wrote a small biography of my grandfather and placed it in my autobiography.

Most people do not encourage members of their family to become biographers. There is no telling what trouble they will get into. If you write fiction, any member of your family who appears on the pages of your book will be hidden by a different name that prevents them being recognised. But biographers are always invading other people's families uninvited, writing about the dead who cannot answer them and presenting what they have written to their subjects' families and friends. It's no surprise we are not welcome.

I was fortunate in never being at a university, going instead to the public library for my education. In the library I found hundreds of possible subjects lined up in alphabetical order and waiting to be chosen. There they all were: Dickens, Shakespeare, Samuel Johnson, Hugh Kingsmill. Which one would you have chosen? I chose the last one. He seemed to have something the others didn't have: an absence of biographies about him (though he wrote some biographies himself – all of them safely out of print). He was, I thought, an obvious choice.

I finished my biography of him within two years – keeping alive doing odd jobs and writing reviews of other people's biographies. Over the next two years I sent my typescript to sixteen publishers who sent it back to me with polite letters. They thanked me for sending it to them and implied that they would have very much liked to publish it, but unfortunately couldn't. They were sorry – and so was I. Sorrow filled the air. But eventually it was taken by someone who had recently given up publishing: Martin Secker. He was, someone told me by way of explanation, almost blind. Mine was the last book he published in his life and he did so with a colleague. It was brought out in 1964 by the Unicorn Press and I was given a generous advance of £25. This came in useful when Kingsmill's second wife objected to a couple of pages in which she appeared and I paid for the rewriting. This rare first edition revealed that it was 'the strange and mysterious quality of her silences which exerted so compelling a power'. I wish she had been more silent with me.

I was gradually learning the complexities of biography, which was almost as difficult as my grandfather's tea making. My father, if asked, would say that I was a historian, which sounded more respectable. He could not see how I would make a financial career from writing and wished I had become a scientist. If I had a proper career I could, he said, write people's lives on Sundays – and, if absolutely necessary, on Saturdays too. What more could I need?

As it was, one of the publishers that had amiably turned down my Kingsmill suggested I should try someone else – preferably someone not unknown but not yet written about. Such subjects are hard to find, I discovered, but eventually I came up with Lytton Strachey. He was a biographer without a biography. What could be better? Indeed he was so good a choice that I was given twice the £25 advance for my first biography. But since it took me seven years to complete the book, I had to renegotiate this part of my contract as many times as Britain negotiated joining – and then leaving – Europe.

In one of his essays the Bloomsbury art critic Clive Bell had written after Strachey's death in 1932 that it would be impossible to write his biography for a long time. It certainly took me a long time to write his life – though that was not what Bell had in mind. In the early 1960s homosexuality was still illegal. It was brave of some of Strachey's friends to talk to me about this. 'Shall I be put in jail?' one of them asked. 'Will I be allowed to watch cricket any more at Lord's?' asked another. It seems ridiculous now, and it was fortunate that the law changed shortly before my biography was published in 1967. Some of the most charming readers of the book were men who invited me to dinner – but were disappointed.

What involved me most deeply was Strachey's extraordinary relationship with Dora Carrington. Though my biographies usually have a man's name on the title page, women take over many chapters. This was inevitably true with my next subject, the artist Augustus John. Walking along the streets of Chelsea in London he sometimes patted the heads of children in case, he explained, 'they are some of mine'.

Sometimes I'm asked how I choose the people whose biographies I write. And I have no idea – no memory of choosing any of them. The fact is, as it were, they choose me, or to put it another way, a minor character in one book gets my attention and becomes my next subject. When I began writing about Ellen Terry (having got to know her when working on my life of Bernard Shaw), I had no intention of writing about her fellow actor on the stage, Henry Irving – but it was impossible to leave him out. And not leaving him out opened the door to both his and her children. So what had begun as a single short pen portrait of one person expanded into a group biography covering two generations over a hundred years. No one was more surprised than me.

Am I writing a biography now? Certainly not! But anything may appear on the next page. I know very little about the next page until it becomes my last page. This is a new sensation. What can it mean? My literary agent tells me that I have suddenly started writing fiction.

Play It Again, Sam

In praise of forgetfulness

I can't recall now who said: 'I've a grand memory for forgetting,' but I know quite well what was meant. The thread of our memories is hung out with clues to our identities, and the manner with which they deceive us shows why a good memory may become essential for a successful career built on telling lies.

But there are also many advantages, I believe, to be had from possessing a poor memory. I can't of course come up, here and now, with all of them, but as a writer of so-called non-fiction, I have been obliged to struggle through virtually the same research again and again, and that has apparently been of considerable benefit to me. I eventually gain, it seems, such an inescapable and unblinking intimacy with the material that I take on the air of a genuine scholar. So, you see, it's really quite useful.

Reference books, when I can lay my hands on them, are the external tools of my memory. All you need is some working knowledge of the alphabet to unlock, like a code, all kinds of recondite information – most of it quite useless. The closing of a reference book, I find, is a very liberating act. Besides, I can always rely on other people – readers, friends and other writers (especially other writers) to help out. They finish my sentences for me and issue corrections freely. On the whole, people like to know better and know more than their friends, I have discovered, so my poor memory has made me unexpectedly popular – more popular than I would have been had I retained more information myself and heaped it on to them. As it is, I am continually impressed by other people's feats of retrieval, sometimes going back hours, and I never fail to congratulate them.

I am told that I must have forgotten so much of my childhood because I lived when young in a state of anxiety. It has been good to forget all this, quite good and rather sensible I think. Now that I am rapidly heading towards my second childhood, I am preparing for a similar exercise in forgetfulness. Moments of pain, humiliation and embarrassment will fall easily away and disappear over the horizon. It's really quite a satisfactory prospect, in fact very satisfactory, and I recommend it to you all.

But it is when I am watching old films on television that my lack of memory is most dramatically brought home to me. I sit on the very edge of my chair, eyes wide, missing nothing, I like to think, and so absorbed in the story that I forget myself – which is a great boon. I love violent films best – I find they calm me, calm my suppressed anxieties, I daresay.

'What are you doing?' my wife suddenly asks me.

Is it a trick question, I wonder? Maggie is afflicted with a tremendously good memory. She knows many poems by Wordsworth, Yeats and others by heart, as well as long speeches from Shakespeare and the entire plots of many novels. It's really quite impressive – on second thoughts *very* impressive. But I am not burdened in this way.

So what am I doing? It seems quite clear to me, but I am rather ashamed of my taste in television films, so I answer vaguely, almost diffidently, even defensively. 'It's unusual, this thriller,' I say. 'Come and watch it. I'm curious to see how it ends. You might like it – I think it's a classic, at any rate quite original.'

'But you've already seen it.'

'I have?'

'Yes. You've seen it a couple of times. The last time was only a month ago.'

'You're joking!' I look back at the screen, anxious not to miss anything.

'I wish I were joking. You said you didn't much like it last time.'

This, I have to confess, surprises me. But perhaps it's someone else she's thinking of. Or perhaps I liked it the first time I saw it. Who can tell? I try out a variation of my defensive play.

'I don't think it is quite like the one we saw. Maybe it is the same director. In any case, this is the director's cut, so it isn't exactly the same. I'd just like to see what happens.'

'What happens is that…'

'Don't tell me! I don't want you to spoil it.'

But it is too late. I've already lost the plot – which means, of course, that sometime or other I can see it again.

I switch off the television and open a book instead. It reads very freshly and there's lot of it: twelve translated volumes in a rather battered light-blue binding. Maggie says it's one of my favourites. So I should enjoy it.

A Legendary Guide

At the next Olympics, watch out for the name Noel Rochford. I would back him against anyone to win a few gold medals. His speciality is what he modestly calls 'walking' – what the rest of us might think of as desperate cross-country marathons. But his day job, a gentle indoor business, seems to be writing 'countryside guides' – particularly guides to the Canary Islands.

My wife and I have developed a habit of taking our summer holidays in February. In four hours' or so flying time from London, or three days' boat journey from Cádiz, you can reach these Isles of the Blessed – La Gomera, El Hierro, La Palma – from any of which you may take a ferry or hydrofoil or catch one of the tiny local planes that the airline, Binter, runs between the islands. But on whichever island you land, you will need a guide. Our guide has been Noel Rochford.

We have never met him. But at moments of extreme exhaustion, lying on some rock or crater at end of day, he has seemed to appear before my eyes as if urging me on to my destination or my doom. Maggie has told me that in my delirium I have sometimes cried out the name 'Noel! Noel!' as if warning innocent travellers that Christmas is about to descend on them again – a frightening prospect in February. Nevertheless I am sure I have seen him several times in the hazy distance. For who else could that far-off figure poised like a god at the very top of an impossible mountain on the inhospitable island of Graciosa be? And what else was that object moving terrifically across the turquoise waters of a strange lagoon on Lobos – what else but the man who wrote so charmingly about that tiny island of anthills, sand dunes and rocky mounds lying between Fuerteventura and Lanzarote?

Noel Rochford is an inviting writer. He has obviously enjoyed his extraordinary athletic feats and writes of them with a dangerous lack of ostentation. It is as if all his life he has outpaced others and walked alone – and now wants us to join him. And we would like to join him. But there lies the difficulty. How can we ever catch up? All time is relative and his time is certainly never my time. I calculate that the 'two hours' or more sinisterly 'under three hours' he notes in his books are the equivalent of my dawn-to-dusk experiences. As I get older – what I would call 'more experienced' – I begin to notice that he is getting quicker on his feet. Whenever he mentions that a walk is 'short', calls an ascent 'gentle', or uses the word 'easy', my advice is to pack for the day. Most of us will never get far enough, I reckon, to reach and enjoy one of his ambitious picnics on the edge of a volcano or under a towering waterfall. These places are all 'unfrequented', he promises – and for very good reasons, it seems to me. I have reconciled myself to taking their beauty, so well concealed within a bleak, imposing landscape, on trust.

According to Noel Rochford, Tenerife, La Palma and Gran Canaria offer the most 'challenging' prospects for 'serious walkers'. So when we visited these last two islands I persuaded Maggie to hire a car – which was quite sufficiently challenging for us both. But on the 'little dome-shaped island' of La Gomera we did walk. It doesn't have that 'barren' and 'unappealing' landscape to the south of Tenerife, which we could see rising impressively out of the sea and which Rochford quixotically recommends as 'ideal for walking'. Nevertheless La Gomera is, as he claims, a walker's paradise. 'Perhaps unawares you will find yourself drawn deeper and deeper into the countryside,' he writes. I cannot deny that there is truth in this and, if you double his timescales, the 'peace and quiet' he describes does begin to envelop you. All the same, watch out for what he painfully calls the 'leg-stretching breaks' of his picnic settings.

The two most popular and crowded islands in the archipelago are Fuerteventura and Lanzarote. But explore these islands with

Noel Rochford and you will see almost no one except an occasional lonely figure disappearing ahead of you. Sometimes I have come across bones scattered along these pitiless routes and wondered whether they belonged to some of his more dedicated followers.

He likens Fuerteventura to the Sahara desert, a thirsty and severe expanse. Tourism suddenly struck this island in the early 1990s. But these tourists, stretched out along its spacious white beaches, seem (except for the bicyclists) to confine themselves to bathing and surfing. 'In case you get tired of beaches' Noel Rochford is ready to entice you inland, where you will find remote villages and crumbling Guanche settlements among the 'old worn hills'. There is, he suggests, 'quite a bit of walking to be enjoyed ... walks to suit all appetites' and he points to the 'rocky *barrancos* [abrupt declivities] in which to flounder'. But I really don't see Noel Rochford floundering. He skims, he flies and he accelerates.

I was pleased to read that he felt that he was 'doing penance' when his publisher first sent him to Lanzarote. 'If you were to suggest walking on Lanzarote to most visitors, they would think you mad,' he admits. But he is not like most people. He is the consummate optimist, driven, wherever he finds himself, to find fresh evidence to nourish his adventurous good spirits. He looks across the dark moon-like rubble of the land with its motionless and impassable streams of jagged lava, like a turbulent and terrifying ocean suddenly frozen as in a nightmare: and behold, it is transformed into an 'alluring' landscape, 'rural and unspoilt'. The vast volcanic eruption that is Lanzarote – the largest in recorded history – no longer appears a threatening and hazardous spectacle. With Rochford as your companion it becomes an exciting place to go exploring.

I have sometimes cried out in anguish to our invisible guide. Does he hear us? Who can say? He walks in mysterious ways and we stumble after him as best we may. I never blamed him when I had my knee operation and nor did Maggie when she was obliged to have her feet treated with electric shocks. I do not class him with the major deities of travel writing like Patrick Leigh Fermor or Colin Thubron. But he is our own guide, our district philosopher and, we pray, our friend.

Charleston Nights

According to Giles Lytton Strachey

I never believed in life after death – and really I was right. My ghostly existence over the last ninety years or so is not what I would call life. There is no sex in this afterlife – just memories and lies, particularly lies. But I like coming back at night to Charleston, where I read a lot. To my surprise I see that the 'Bloomsberries', as they like to call us, are still having new books published all the time – letters and diaries mostly. No wonder Virginia's reputation had soared so high: her non-fiction was always better than her novels, don't you think? Many of us, too, have been the subjects of biographies written by what I call academic journalists. My biography is so long that my own books are lost in it. I forget the man's name – something like Holmes or Ackroyd.

Charleston is by far the best destination for me and for the other Bloomsberries too. Our houses and homes in the country or at Gordon Square have been destroyed or changed out of all recognition. Charleston is essentially the same. It is amazing to think that it is a hundred years since Vanessa decided to move in – that is much older than I am (we don't go on counting our years after death – there seems no point). What is special about Charleston is that it has a past, a present and a mysterious future, one leading naturally to the other. When I come here at night I feel at home, seeing so much that is familiar to me. I see many friends – indeed the place is packed with them – Duncan, Vanessa, Clive and all their lovers and rivals. They are in the pictures and the books and also in my mind. This is a living past. I still silently laugh when I remember Maynard's experiment with time at Charleston. It is extraordinary how foolish clever people can be. He insisted on altering the clocks there so that they were an hour ahead of summer time during the summer of 1920. The result was complete confusion. It was like a Chekhov play in which everyone laughs and screams and passes on. It was drama without tragedy.

I first came to stay at Charleston in 1917. For some reason Vanessa thought Carrington and I were trying to make the Barn into a new home for us. Certainly I had no such idea. But I remember climbing Firle Beacon in brilliant sunlight, looking over the Downs, then across the sea, and thinking how marvellous the country was. It has not changed in a hundred years.

Though Maynard wrote *The Economic Consequences of the Peace* here and Clive struggled with his art criticism, I found it almost impossible to write at Charleston. It was a wonder I ever finished the last of my *Eminent Victorians*, poor old General Gordon. There was so much going on all the time: parties, picnics, country walks, amateur dramas, children playing in the garden and falling into the pond, music on the gramophone and, late into the night, streams of fascinating gossip. I never tired of that. No wonder I found it hard to do anything but chatter.

Looking round now, I see that the whole house is painted so that anyone who steps inside becomes part of a Bloomsbury picture. Charleston itself was Duncan's and Vanessa's masterpiece. They painted all the day when they were not in each other's arms – and suddenly, far too late, I see why Carrington may well have wanted to live in the Barn. The whole place was a litter of easels and paintboxes, palettes, brushes and turpentine and tubes of paint. Carrington was never happier than in the company of other painters who talked about their work and other people's. She did not have that when living with me. I've heard a rumour that a book of her letters is to be published next year and this I think will please her. It will take the place of David Garnett's edition of them, which excludes her happy years at the Slade School of Fine Art, where she learnt to paint.

Enter the house now and you appear to be where the Bloomsbury Group are still living and working. Actually it is an original museum and a centre for literature, the theatre, music and art. From November to mid-March each year I have the place largely to myself and the spirits of my past friends, two generations of them. Then, just when I am feeling a little lonely, a little bored, visitors pour in from all over Britain and abroad. They go from room to room, from the bedrooms to the studio and out into the beautiful garden. In the shop they buy all sorts of attractive crockery and vases as well as postcards and clothes. There are also books – I must take a look and see if mine are there.

But the main events of the summer are the two Charleston festivals. The newest is dedicated to the short story, which always needs help; I like it because I like anything that is short – in books I mean, not other things: quite the opposite. The chief festival takes place in the summer. There is a large tent at the end of the garden and one of the barns is also used. There are readings, debates, interviews and even one-act plays some-times taken from Bloomsbury letters. But, thank God (actually that's not a phrase we use where I am), mercifully the events are never restricted to Bloomsbury. One of the most popular performances was an actress called Eileen Atkins using Ellen Terry's little book on the triumphant and pathetic women in Shakespeare's plays, as well as the letters they wrote and the children they had. I feared there would be no humour in it, but it was captivating and reminded me that once upon a time I wanted to be a playwright.

The money that has been spent on Charleston has not ruined it with that awful modernist architecture. By making repairs to what-ever had come apart and renewing what had faded, it has brought the past into the present and the present into the past. It is as if time does not exist. But a few months ago I heard of something called the Centenary Project which gave me the shudders. Why can't people leave things as they are? The answer here is that there have been two calamities. In the 1960s the eighteenth-century Granary was demolished to make way for large tractors; and in the 1980s there was a fire that seriously damaged the Hay Barn. I remember that fire, it caught my attention and seeing the flames I thought I was back in my afterlife home. The new project is to repair these barns, restoring their historical fabric. There will be a larger court-yard and a new café. I have to admit that it reads as an imaginative and useful plan. But I shall have to see how words are translated into facts before I give my judgement.

All at Sea

My story goes back to the summer of 2001 when my wife and I sailed to New York on the *QE2*. We had worked our passages across the Atlantic a couple of times before, giving talks on art and literature in return for first-class accommodation. The talks themselves were hazard events depending on special weather: no wind and much rain. When the sun shone the passengers preferred to sit on deck drinking cocktails, practising golf swings and tennis serves behind a net or plunging into the pool – almost anything rather than listen to a discourse on 'Landscape and Literature'. If the wind and the rain were violent, we usually began with a better audience but, as we clung for balance to our lectern, it would unsteadily diminish as one of us was speaking, the passengers lurching away with horrible groans down to the privacy of their bunks. Once I gave a lecture as best I could while lying on a padded chaise longue, an invaluable piece of stage furniture.

Even in perfect weather there are sudden risks: a titanic rush to port or starboard if, for instance, a fleet of dolphins is spotted, leaving 'Wordsworth and the Lake District' deserted.

There were always other lecturers at sea with broader agendas – often a seafaring gentleman who spoke knowledgeably on 'Voyages of Discovery'. Most popular of all was Sir Bernard Ingham, who communicated anecdotes from his days as chief press secretary to Margaret Thatcher, brilliantly orchestrating moments of operatic melodrama with pauses for intimate chuckling. All these proved successful counter-attractions to our own offerings.

But our last voyage that summer was a very different business –
a voyage of discovery. We were speaking to a group of approximately fifty Americans who, following a tour of Britain, were
returning to the United States. We had, in the best sense, a captive
audience, which had such perfect manners that they seemed to
prefer sitting indoors with us each morning to promenading the
decks, with all their attractions.

We were curious to see how the other speakers were getting
on. There was one who appeared to be speaking all the time and
whose name was faintly familiar to us both: Paul Burrell. Hadn't
we read about him in the newspapers? Wasn't he accused of
making off with some of Diana, Princess of Wales's silverware –
perhaps her jewellery? We thought it possible. But it was hardly
likely that someone due to appear in Her Majesty's criminal court
in the autumn would be appearing on a ship named after Her
Majesty in the summer. Nevertheless the lecturer was billed as
being a royal footman or butler. So what would he be speaking
about? We decided to find out.

Paul Burrell appeared well suited; the shirt correctly ironed, the
careful tie properly in place, the shoes slightly gleaming. Nothing
excessive. Nothing much. I thought this rather brave of him. He
took up a fork and showed it to us. It was, he said, a fork. Would
he bend it like Uri Geller? Or, like a conjuror, make it disappear?
But he did nothing of that sort. Instead, he placed the fork on a
table as you or I might do. He placed it down with tremendous
deliberation, moving it to the left of where a plate gently rested.

'This is,' he said, 'a fork.' He explained what he was doing. 'I am
putting the fork on the table exactly where a member of the royal
family would expect to find it at luncheon or dinner.' He mentioned
a special distance – half an inch this way, half an inch that way. He
smiled down at it and then across at us. I was mesmerised. Where
could this be leading? What would happen next?

What happened next was the placing of a knife. It was the
same, only different. It was parallel to the fork but not next to
it – that was very important. It was on the other side of the plate:
in short, the right side of the plate. A fearful symmetry was being
built up – gradually, over six days at sea. Not only cutlery was

involved in this architecture – there were wine and water glasses, napkins, plates of differing sizes all to be controlled. All items were arranged in their exactitude on the table, put there with loving care. Could this really be happening in the mid-Atlantic? An inexplicable astonishment grew in me.

I was not the only person so affected. One gentleman rose to his feet and excitedly asked how the queen ate a banana. We all leant forward and watched intently as Paul Burrell, brilliantly bringing both hands into play, and employing some of the cutlery, demonstrated the art of royal banana-eating. It was a virtuoso performance and in less than ten minutes of unhesitating explanation, he had completed it. We sat back and gasped, never having realised before what eating such complex fruit as a banana should be.

With difficulty we tore ourselves away. But that evening in our cabin, I turned on the television and saw that Paul Burrell's lecture had been recorded. There he stood with the fork, the knife and the table, his loyal companions, like people in a fairy tale, condemned to be placed on this table for ever. My wife switched it off, but I begged to see it one more time. I was of such little faith that I simply could not credit it. I had to see it again that night and the next night to make sure I had not been dreaming.

Some of our American audience had gone to hear Burrell in the afternoon, and I was eager to find out what they thought of him. To sustain such a minimum of action over such an eloquent period struck them as unusual. 'He was quite professional,' said one of them – adding unexpectedly: 'It was almost pure farce.'

And yet when had farce ever been played with such solemnity? I felt Paul Burrell had invented a new theatrical genre, a precious blend of poignancy and pomp. It seemed a pity that he could not play it later from the dock. But one of our Americans was critical. She had seen the film *Gosford Park* on board the *QE2* and did not think that Paul Burrell came up to the standard of the servants in it. 'I would have thought the queen could have afforded someone better,' she said. Perhaps, I thought, she was referring to his appearance. He was like a middleweight pugilist learning ballet. But this criticism belonged to the world of

P. G. Wodehouse, where a gentleman's gentleman is always far superior to the gentleman himself.

Unlike some others, Paul Burrell has been scrupulous never to claim superiority over his royal employers. That would be a grave error. He went out of the way to show that he was merely their equal.

My Identity Crisis

More than a hundred years ago the word 'bank' referred to a grassy slope. Only in the twentieth century did it refer to money houses. How straightforward life must have been once upon a time.

Unfortunately I was out the morning my bank rang. A woman's voice asked me to call back, but the number was engaged all afternoon. I didn't worry. Her voice had sounded so casual and relaxed I knew it couldn't be urgent. She had rattled off her phone number with such joyful speed I was able to take down only one digit each of the seven times I played her message back.

When I phoned the next day a man answered. The woman who had been attempting to contact me, he said, worked part-time and I wouldn't be able to reach her until the following week. 'What did you want to speak to her about?' he asked. This was a more difficult question than it sounded. 'I don't know,' I replied. There was a pause. 'Then I'm not sure I can help you,' he volunteered. We were in a cul-de-sac. So I took a deep breath and explained – which led us to a familiar obstacle course. Who was my mother, when was I born, what was my password, my code, my number, the first and last lines of my address?

'Would you please hold on,' I was asked, when all this had been completed. I was left listening to some music.

The music was interrupted by another man's voice. 'This is fraud,' he announced. For a moment I thought he had said Fred. 'Have you been in touch with the bank recently?'

'I tried yesterday,' I said apologetically, 'but without luck.'

'I meant did you speak to us in the last three or four days?'

'Not so far as I can recall. Three or four days – that's a long time.'

'You haven't ordered a new bank card?'

'No. Mine is working fine, thank you.'

'Not any more it isn't. We cancelled it yesterday after we posted your new one. Did you lose your card?'

'No. I have it here in front of me.'

'Then I advise you to cut it up into small pieces.'

Apparently someone using my name had phoned the bank, said he had lost his/my bank card and ordered another. He gave my mother's name, the date of my birth and verified my address where he asked the card to be posted. The bank sent it, but I had not received it – and never would. Apparently there were four similar cases in the neighbourhood. This pointed to someone working for the Royal Mail as the culprit, I was told, and the fraud department at the bank was making elaborate plans to catch her – or him. It was going to post me another card in an obvious and inviting bank envelope. So if I received nothing that was good news because … At this point I interrupted.

It did not seem good news to me. If I scissored my useless bank-card and did not receive another, how was I to get money from the local branch of my bank or pay some of my bills? Fred from the fraud squad (as I came to think of him) admitted that this might be troublesome. But it wouldn't last for ever, he reassured me. In three or four months perhaps normal service would be resumed. Until then I must not use any telephone or online banking. And I would have to take my passport, driving licence and other proofs of who I am to the bank before I cashed a cheque. The first time I did this, the woman at the till was obliged to go through a compli-cated conversation with the fraud department herself, while a long line of customers gathered impatiently behind me. I think she quite enjoyed this conversation – anyway she was polite enough to say it had added to her work experience and interrupted the monotony of her routine business. But for the rest us on the other side of the counter it was a bad half-hour and some of them, hear-ing the word 'fraud', looked at me with suspicion.

Things, I decided, could not go on like this. So I phoned Fred –
and he suggested that I get on to the Royal Mail fraud office. I did
this – but was eventually told that my bank did not use the Royal
Mail. So I phoned Fred again. He was surprised by this news,
but said that the fraud department had no contact with the post
department of the bank. In which case, I replied, how did he know
that someone in the post department of his bank was not responsible for my mail being taken. 'I very much hope that's not the
case,' he said. 'And I very much hope that the case can be sorted
out quickly,' I replied.

Since most of my security procedures could be easily found
from reference books and on the Internet, we decided that all
this must be changed. My mother now has a different name; I
have acquired a younger brother and chosen a favourite television
programme that I loved as a child (when there was no television).
In short, I have a virtual life. The one thing I asked for – a new
birthday – has for some reason (and with much laughter) been
denied. I would have liked to claw back twenty years or been
given an impressive new seniority. My main worry with my new
identity is that I will forget who I am.

Barbara Smoker's Ninetieth Birthday

Barbara Smoker, now in her very young nineties, has seen a good deal of what I call active service. I refer not to her three or four years during the early 1940s when she was a wireless telegraphist in the Women's Royal Naval Service in South-East Asia but to the rest of her career, which has been full to overflowing with active service. Born into a Roman Catholic family and educated in a convent, she fought her way out and, at the age of twenty-six, joined the ranks of the secular humanist army. She was to take part in many vigorous campaigns: campaigns against the Vietnam War and the death penalty, campaigns in favour of embryo research, legal abortion and voluntary euthanasia. She has travelled to India and the United States promoting atheism – and was herself promoted to the rank of president of the National Secular Society. This is a very short and selective account of what I call her war record. In fact she is a pacifist who has never ceased fighting. Seldom does she have time for sleep, which she regards as a rather silly indulgence. She has a clear and precise mind and lives, I believe, in utter chaos, the springs of her mattress having, in Smokeresque fashion, fought their way through to its surface. In 2005, at the Sorbonne, she was presented with an award by the International Humanist and Ethical Society. This may be compared to a Military Cross given for pronounced bravery combined with a Distinguished Service Medal for a lifetime's achievement. She combines courage and tenacity.

I came to know Barbara through our joint interest in Bernard Shaw. As Shaw's authorised biographer, I take it upon myself to say that there has never been a more genuine, more formidable, more terrific Shavian than Barbara. When I published a symposium on Shaw in the late 1970s I called on her to contribute an essay that no one else could have written with such expert knowledge and passionate commitment. Her contribution was called 'The Man of Letters' and it dealt with Shaw's belief in the value of a new phonetic 'alfabet' and the great legal battle over his last will and testament.

Shaw had wanted the money from his estate for the first twenty-one years after his death to be used for the creation and distribution of this new alphabet. But two of the residuary legatees, the Royal Academy of Dramatic Art and the British Museum, did not want to wait so long before becoming themselves financial beneficiaries of Shaw's will. So they took a case against the 'alfabet' on the grounds that the trust in its favour was not legally charitable.

In Jarndyce v. Jarndyce fashion it was the best part of six years following Shaw's death before this case reached the Chancery Court, by which time Barbara Smoker was thirty-two and becoming a seasoned campaigner. She was already effective in all sorts of public ways, learning much from another Shavian enthusiast, Eric Batson, a librarian and actor who was to form a useful 'Not Bloody Likely' committee. But there was a difference between them: Batson was an eccentric who came up with some brilliant original ideas; Barbara was an original who, to some people, appeared to be an eccentric with a gift for paradox. She lived in two attic rooms without indoor sanitation on Catford Hill, eating very little meat and buying her clothes at jumble sales. She had no regular office job, no obvious professional career, but made a modest living by writing some challenging journalism and by winning competitions – literary competitions in papers and magazines, and competitions for slogans and jingles on the backs of tins and packets.

She had no job, but she was always busy. On Thursdays, for example, she could be heard on her soapbox at Tower Hill contradicting what the Methodist minister Donald Soper had been saying on Wednesdays. Much of the week would be taken up by her chairmanship of the Family Squatting Movement, her work for the Radical Alternatives to Prison Committee, and her dual role as secretary of the Phonetic Alphabet Association and assistant secretary to the Shaw Society. In these latter roles she was determined to support the validity of Shaw's will. But Shaw's solicitors and the Public Trustee, who represented Shaw's estate, refused to tell her when and exactly where the court hearing was to take place. So she went to the court, made a friend there, and telephoned him every day.

Listening from the public gallery to the mellifluous opening speeches of the bewigged barristers, it took her several minutes to grasp the fact that, being profoundly ignorant of phonetics, they were mouthing pure poppycock. As the only person in court who had this vital knowledge, it was crucial that she come to the aid of the learned counsel before it was too late. And so, when the case adjourned for the day, she approached the Attorney General's team – and no one could throw her off.

The following day she descended from the public gallery into the body of the court and into the thick of the battle, where she set about demolishing the residuary legatees' arguments. In a postscript to my biography of Shaw I describe her amassing thousands of potent words each day and slipping them into the barrister's briefcase. She filled it with facts about everything from shorthand and Morse code to the relative frequency of English speech sounds and the educational use of phonetic lettering. She was horrified by the court's ignorance, but pleased, at the end of the week, when counsel opened his tremendously bulging brief-case and she looked into its jaws, and saw most of the material there was from her.

Shaw's team did not win the case, but Barbara Smoker had given them enough to justify an appeal. Unfortunately this appeal never came to court but led to an out-of-court compromise, which allowed a little over £8,000 of Shaw's money to be paid to the prospective 'alfabet'. Barbara felt disgusted by this outcome. It was a pitiful sum of money considering the wildly success-ful opening of *My Fair Lady*. She was, and is, a no-compromise woman; she is after absolutes.

And she has achieved many. Over the next half-century and more, she continued with her campaigns: producing strings of verse with which to tie up the deity and witty anti-Christmas cards each December; also conducting gay and lesbian weddings, and appearing on television as she was knocked to the ground when carrying a 'free speech' banner in support of Salman Rushdie.

When Shaw was ninety he was interviewed by a young journalist from the local newspaper. At the end of the interview the young man thanked Shaw and said he hoped to interview G. B. S. again on his hundredth birthday. 'I don't see why not,' Shaw replied. 'You look pretty well to me.'

I cannot guarantee how many of us here will be able to celebrate Barbara's hundredth birthday. But I feel certain that she will see more of her campaigns (such as voluntary euthanasia) passed into law before she reaches her centenary.

A Knight of the Sorrowful Countenance

This is the saddest picture I ever saw. It was commissioned, among more cheerful portraits, by Sir Christopher Ondaatje, one of the patrons of British art, who planned to open a unique literary museum in an early-nineteenth-century farmhouse (to which a laundry extension had been added in the 1850s). This building is set a little above his home in the remote cliffs near Countisbury on the north Devon coast and was once used to service it. The refurbished fabric of the farmhouse has now become the setting for his gallery-museum. He has filled it with books by writers past and present, accompanied by their portraits in a variety of forms – photographs, bronze and marble busts, charcoal drawings, watercolours, oils, copies of original paintings and new portraits of living writers by members of the Royal Society of Portrait Painters. It is an extraordinary *omnium gatherum.*

One artist taking on this challenge was Michael Reynolds, who had won the Ondaatje Prize for Portraiture in 2003. He wrote to me from Italy asking whether he might come and paint me when he was next in England during the spring of 2007. I hesitated before agreeing. Portrait painters, after all, must rely on the cooperation of sitters in much the same way as biographers rely on the help of all those who occupy their acknowledgement pages.

There are people who view having one's portrait painted as an exercise in vanity – and for some celebrity portraiture perhaps this is true. But for me it is a disturbing experience. When I work, trying to build up pen portraits within a biographical narrative, the flow of energy goes from me towards my subjects. I lose myself while concentrating on them and, all being well, I feel much better after this holiday from myself. But when sitting for a portrait the current of energy travels in the opposite direction, what feels to me the wrong direction. It is difficult to be natural. Is that rictus of a smile, which has become fixed across my face, natural? Or am I behaving like a tame animal trying to please? I would prefer to close my eyes, hiding part of myself. That would seem more natural – but also rather rude. To talk or not to talk? That is the question.

Michael Reynolds wanted to talk and wanted me to talk. He arrived for a preliminary inspection the day before our sittings began and told me that, several years before, he had reviewed my life of Augustus John and it was this which had decided him to choose me as a subject. As with John, drawing lay at the heart of all his work, including what Brian Sewell described as 'the stout and studied portraits of his later years'. I noticed he looked at none of the pictures on my walls. He was here to inspect the rooms and see what was best for his work. The dining room with its blue wallpaper got the morning light and he choose this for our sessions, which were to take place in the afternoons. Settling himself tightly in a corner with his back to the window, he put up his easel between us, placed the empty canvas on it, and left it there for the night. Each sitting over the next four days was to last some four hours, with an interval for tea.

Michael Reynolds was a couple of years older than me and approaching his mid-seventies with caution interrupted by spasms of irritation. Like me he had come through a serious operation for cancer, and was soon pressing various recipes upon me, asserting the merits of some magic drops of an untranslatable Dutch substance that had come highly recommended by a Lebanese doctor he had met in Spain. I envied him his fierce and fantastical optimism.

I sat in a solitary upright chair facing his corner encampment and we began talking. Brought up in Brighton and educated at Brighton College of Art, he had taught intermittently at various art schools and in the early 1960s gone for a year or two to Rome, having won an engraving scholarship at the British School there. After his return, he opened a wine shop in Norfolk and had become, he assured me, quite a scholar of vintages. He had been married and had four daughters, but he did not strike me as a family man. He was gregarious but solitary. When he spoke of his achievements it was less as an artist than a cook: his slowly prepared basmati rice, his 'heavenly loaves' of wholemeal bread ('brown and crusty like granny's dream world') and, best of all, his triumphant chestnut soup with its lavish fresh-ground pepper and the juice of a lemon. No salt.

On matters of art he brimmed over with formidable opinions. No woman should seriously think of taking up painting – she would simply be wasting her time. There were of course a few exceptions to this rule – Artemisia Gentileschi, Mary Cassatt, Gwen John – but no others came to mind. He himself had mathematical rules for portraiture, measuring the size of a canvas and placing the head with formal discipline upon it. This was how the old masters worked – very far from 'the flabby canvases' that had become fashionable in the late twentieth century.

In 1977 he had won the *Sunday Times* Landscape Into Art prize and been elected to the Royal Society of Portrait Painters. But though he became proficient in what was curiously called 'skilled art', his accomplished landscapes, still lifes, nudes and portraits were seen as belonging to a chapter in the history of art that was long past. His contempt for all experimental and abstract work had sometimes reminded people of that most outspoken opponent of modern art, the late president of the Royal Academy, Sir Alfred Munnings. But the Royal Academy had changed since Munnings's day, and though Michael Reynolds often exhibited there, he felt more at home as a member of the Royal Society of Portrait Painters, earning his income mainly with commissioned portraits (there are examples of his work at the National Portrait Gallery and in the Royal Collection).

To win a place for more traditional contemporary pictures, he founded, with the support of Brian Sewell, the Discerning Eye exhibitions in 1989. This was a successful innovation of annual open-submission shows restricted to small paintings and sculpture, the dimensions of which were strictly limited. The exhibits were selected by a mixed panel of collectors, artists and critics whose independent judgement would be clear for all to see. By the mid-1990s, however, after a series of rows over some panellists' choices (Michael Reynolds believed that to gain publicity the collectors were being replaced by celebrities), he angrily resigned and, in despair over the British art scene, exiled himself. By the time he wrote to me he been mainly living abroad for a decade, exhibiting his work in Europe and dividing his time between Italy, which he loved, and Holland, where he was looked after by a married couple.

Michael Reynolds, as I soon discovered, was very well read. But he had little good to say about most twentieth-century writers with the exception of Iain M. Banks and Patricia Highsmith. He challenged me to come up with some good new authors, and so we began an animated conversation. I had the feeling that he wanted me to persuade him to take a more buoyant view of contemporary writing and with it perhaps of contemporary life. That, at any rate, is what I found myself doing. For though he was oddly optimistic about his esoteric medicines and had plenty of energy, his judgements were imbued with a belligerent pessimism. He appeared to enjoy being in the wilderness – Brian Sewell referred to him as a 'gadfly and maverick ... in every aspect of his life and work an outsider'. But I had the feeling he would have liked to find himself with a more secure and celebrated reputation (providing he did not have to be polite to anyone).

I did not examine the portrait between our sittings since he did not want me to look at it. He grew, I realised, very anxious over his paintings while he was at work on them. The design of my portrait, he declared at the end of our last sitting, was eminently apt, but he needed more time to 'give it intensity'. Since he never painted from photographs, he would welcome a couple more sittings when he returned to England the following year. I hesitantly agreed to this and when he left, heaving the canvas and easel into his car, I gave him a copy of *The Oxford Companion to English Literature* by my wife, Margaret Drabble. I felt rather nervous over his response to this present (particularly as it had a portrait of Vanessa Bell by Duncan Grant on the jacket), but he was delighted, describing it in a letter from Italy as 'a marvellous piece of scholarship in succinct, elegant English'. He was putting it to good use, he added, by picking out names of contemporary writers and firing them off to Ondaatje for inclusion in his 'Elysium hall'.

Over the next few months we exchanged six or eight letters. 'I am sad that the portrait of you is not more developed,' he wrote. 'I don't care that it's distorted since, as I told you, all my work is distorted, but this is concealed given a little more time'. His letters, written in a fine italic hand, were warm-hearted and generous. He thanked me for allowing him to 'reach into your banks of charity' and give him two more sittings, the dates of which we fixed.

In March 2008, shortly before these sittings were to take place and not having heard from him for two or three months, I wrote again and received a reply from his agent informing me that his cancer had returned and spread dramatically. He was in a hospital in Holland where he had been told there was no hope of recovery. 'Michael asked me to send you the following message, especially for you. He is not able to write by hand. We have to do this by email.' His message was set out in short paragraphs.

> The great roulette wheel is about to stop spinning for me and we can all see it ends in zero.
> So, my dear Michael, I bitterly regret I shan't be able to go on playing with your portrait.

He also sent his disappointment at not being able to continue our conversations together.

I had not been greatly looking forward to these extra sittings, but now felt mean about this reluctance and suddenly found myself missing them. A few days later I read an obituary in the *Guardian* by William Packer describing him as 'one of the most naturally gifted painters of his generation ... building up over the years a deserved reputation as a master of the contemporary portrait ... His misfortunes were to a degree much of his own making, for he was a difficult man, irascible, combative ... capable of being formidably offensive.' But, Packer continued, his talent won him the admiration of his peers and his support for work he admired won him their affection. Reading this, I felt he had guided me through the angry entanglements of his personality so that I too had come to feel affection for him.

Six months later I received an invitation from Christopher Ondaatje to attend a private opening of his literary museum on the cliffs of the north Devon coast. It was a bewildering get-together of images and books. The old laundry contains early printing presses, the earliest being a large cast-iron Albion (similar to Caxton's wooden press). They are overlooked by Shakespeare, Milton, Chaucer and other venerable writers. The ground floor of the house is largely given over to the Bloomsbury Group and its associates: Leonard and Virginia Woolf, Lytton Strachey, Maynard Keynes, Joyce, Eliot and members of the Memoir Club. The copy of a well-known Vita Sackville-West portrait shares one corner with an original portrait of the young Violet Trefusis by the Scottish Royal Academician William Rankin. Here and on the first floor the dead keep amiable if unlikely company with the living: Doris Lessing, Pepys, Michael Frayn, Tennyson, the Brontës ... Throughout the museum there are busts of Bernard Shaw, Ian Fleming, Dickens, Arthur C. Clarke, Rossetti and others.

As I climbed the stairs to the first floor, I saw hanging on the wall over the half-landing above me Michael Reynolds's picture. It was a shock. I don't think I have ever seen so melancholy a portrait. I looked away and back again several times, and each time I looked, it appeared more profoundly sorrowful than my immediate memory of it.

The Times obituary had noted that among his most intense paintings while fighting cancer during these last four years were a series of self-portraits. Externally this portrait I am looking at has a resemblance to me, but essentially I believe it to be a concealed self-portrait of the artist. I wondered whether, after another couple of sittings, he might have lightened my expression and I his spirits. In its present state, as if held in limbo, I sense I am a mask through which the painter is looking at the world beyond that corner window where he sat during those cold spring afternoons: one Michael confronting another.

Disappearing

Before I was twenty, death was simply disappearance: someone walking into another room and closing the door; or the stage trick performed by a conjuror, painless and inexplicable, that left audiences knowing that somewhere behind the descending curtain everything was all right.

But during the 1950s my grandfather died. He died upstairs in his bedroom and then downstairs in the room where the family had made up a bed for him. He died on the stairs going down; he died in the ambulance going off; and again in the hospital, once in a ward and two or three times in a private room. It took an awful time, his dying, and we all died a little with him.

I saw it even then as a test for us all. My grandfather was what we called a fine man. There was vague talk of his exploits on the river and the cricket pitch. He was tall, had a neat, prim moustache – and spent much time harmlessly pursuing his spectacles, his teeth, hearing aid and so on. He read *The Times* and he believed what he read – until, that was, he began to die.

During his last twenty years he had a sorry life. Though he had the equipment – gloves, bowler hat and a military umbrella – and carried it all with him to London occasionally in the train, handing his *Times* up to the engine driver when they reached Paddington, he did not comprehend financial business. The post would arrive and he would set to work filling the backs of envelopes with complicated columns of figures. But they never 'came out' as they should have done and he would look up honestly bewildered and accuse his tea of being cold. Once there had been some money, now there was not – no one knew why. The world was changing. He grasped his umbrella and gloves but they did not help. The house was beginning to fall to bits and we lived under a double mortgage. The figures on the envelopes multiplied and there was no solution.

My grandmother's contribution was to complain: this was her privilege and her talent. She never had money – and missed it dreadfully. She looked forward to becoming familiar with it but had no idea how she would get it and what she would do with it. Perhaps she needed money as security, stacked up in the bank to comfort her against the unfocused anxieties that death absorbs. She added to her illusions by using a few French words ('*Jamais!*' was one of them – though as a child I believed it meant confectionery) to enrich her lamentations and the scoldings she gave invisible servants.

There was no day, while I was growing up, no morning or afternoon, no breakfast, lunch or dinner that was not accompanied with quarrels and abuse, and sometimes tears and exits, which accompanied my aunt coming in to control the washing-up. She was, on the whole, an outdoor figure, firmly planted on the grass and among the trees but determined not to let her mother wash the spoons, saucepans or glasses. In despair my grandmother appealed to 'the Almighty' to take her, but he never did while my grandfather was alive.

Ours was the sort of life that encouraged us to entreat death until my grandfather began to die. It was then we realised, all of us, how much better a living death was than a real one. It became a monster in the house. My bedroom window overlooked a cemetery and I would hear the bells ringing over it, 'an open space among the ruins', as Shelley wrote, '… It might make one in love with death, to think that one should be buried in so sweet a place.' It had been so easy to be 'half in love with easeful death', to call the monster soft names and believe it would behave softly.

We had known death as part of fiction; my grandfather brought it to us as fact. His was what is described as a 'natural' death. He died slowly, reluctantly, with desperation and in fear, realising in his exhaustion that there was nowhere to go but into oblivion.

The change in him was awful. His life, for so long incomprehensible and bleak, now seemed to him wonderfully desirable. He yearned for more of it. But the remorselessness of the dying process, which used up all his strength, made him unrecognisable as the man we had turned to at the head of the dining table, who had dominated world affairs with the aid of the wireless but who was now frightened of the nurses. All he had believed, all we had struggled to believe in, like him, was gradually rubbed away in front of us. He had believed: but who could help him now in his disbelief? Of what use were the gentlemanly standards he had followed? All his life he had religiously lost his money and in death he was not rewarded. He had left his card but the Great Gentleman above was not at home.

As a source of strength his vanished faith was replaced with drugs and these also changed him. They made him sleep, but this gave him no rest. His sleep was pitted with nightmares and he would wake, worn out as if he had been wrestling with an unseen opponent. The addition of drugs altered his appearance as the loss of belief altered his character. His face sank and the colour of his skin grew faintly green. The hospital ward was full of men lying at acute angles in barricaded beds, strapped, plugged, tied, suspended, wrapped. Like grotesque babies, they lay in their cots, waiting. One day, after an hour at the bedside, I was relieved by my aunt, who wearily pointed out that I had been sitting next to the wrong patient.

The wards with their marching matrons and implacable sisters were like parade grounds where the 'Last Post' was constantly sounding. The dramatist Dennis Potter told a story of a man opposite him in hospital who was to die of cancer at midday being asked by a doctor earlier that morning how he felt and replying gently, 'In the pink!' That is how it should be done. By such standards my grandfather was not doing well. He feared he was letting us down. This was what he meant when he turned to me and whispered, 'I'm sorry.'

Death is a fragment of democracy. We begin to die when more people begin to prefer us dead. 'We must love one another or die.' We must die. There were times during my grandfather's ordeal when I caught myself willing it to be over. He did not want that, but in the secret ballot he was outvoted. When they telephoned to say that he had died 'peacefully' one morning, all of us felt some relief. But the death in the family is a conveyor belt and a polite 'next, please'.

We all reacted differently. My father looked grave – the kind of face he used going to business meetings. 'My God! This is an awful place,' he said as we stood in the undertaker's hygienic office. My grandmother wrung her hands above her head and sang her grief with an Irish dirge that scraped our nerves and gave us a target for our hostility. My aunt deplored this undignified opera, which seemed to parody her own pain. Her father had been her god: no one could match her sense of loss. We fell back as she came up to the corpse plastered with frozen pink cosmetics, leant over and lingeringly kissed his face. I could not do it: there was too much fear in me.

I tried to write my feelings down later but never reached an end. I raged against the dying of the light. 'I could die today if I wished,' wrote Samuel Beckett, 'merely by making a little effort.' We have come to understand and respect those who take an initiative – John Berryman, Sylvia Plath, Virginia Woolf and others. In London a play on euthanasia was a hit. But to be in control of one's death, how and when, is not easy. For thirty years a friend of mine has been carrying round with him a fatal lozenge, which he will one day pop into his mouth. I admire this, but I have not asked him for one of these lozenges myself.

A Forgotten Gwen John Scholar

During the late 1960s and early 1970s, while I was writing a biography of Augustus John, another writer, Mary Taubman, was pursuing research into the life and work of his sister, Gwen John. We were introduced one evening by Augustus's son Edwin, who was also Gwen's copyright holder. When young, Edwin had been a champion boxer known as Teddy John. But while in Paris, and under Gwen's influence, he turned instead to watercolours. Though there were still signs of the pugilist about him, it was the painter we both knew.

Working in tandem, Mary and I became good friends. We had, it seemed to me, a perfect partnership without any sense of rivalry, any withholding of material. Getting to know the early years of our subjects in Wales and at the Slade School of Fine Art, and being able to talk about them with vicarious intimacy, the isolation of writing such books was diminished. Sometimes there were jokes about us: how Mary was increasingly growing to resemble Gwen; how my style of living was being influenced by Augustus. But such jokes touched us only lightly.

Mary had been a painter. She wrote with a painter's eye, with the tone and precision of a natural writer, a humane scholar. Born in Scotland, she had graduated at Edinburgh University, where she wrote a thesis on Gwen John's work. In 1953, her final year as a student, she went to France to meet Edwin, who, she wrote, 'more than any other person could help or hinder my researches'.

In my opinion he did both. I believe that, in his fashion, he came to love Mary. But he had a sometimes aggressive, sometimes teasing low self-esteem and feared that Mary would not continue to see him once he had shown her all Gwen's archive. Over twenty years, until his death in 1976, he handed her the papers in gentle instalments. Once, she told me, while they were on the top of a bus long after their first meeting, he hesitantly mentioned an interesting batch of Rodin's letters to Gwen, saying that he really must show them to her one day.

I completed my biography in six or seven years – rather a rush it may have seemed to Mary, though perhaps appropriate for Augustus's frenzied life and speedy methods of composition. Her work on Gwen became a lifetime commitment. She was a perfectionist and needed infinite patience to reach her goal. Edwin gave her the time, gave her more than she needed, insisted on it – and in such a generous way that she began to lose momentum. Her research was meticulous and original. She actually walked from Bordeaux, up the Garonne, to Toulouse – the same 'crazy walk' Gwen had undertaken with Augustus's mistress Dorelia in 1903. She published little: mainly introductions to exhibitions at Faerber and Maison, the Arts Council of Great Britain and the Anthony d'Offay Gallery between 1964 and 1976. But such was the quality of her writing that she was seen as the principal authority on Gwen John's work.

Everything changed after Edwin died and Gwen's copyrights passed to his son and daughter. Not perhaps knowing all the circumstances (Mary had lived and worked in France for a time and also taught at the Cardiff College of Art), they became understandably impatient and eventually took back the material Edwin had lent her. Over the next twenty-five years biographies of Gwen by Susan Chitty and Sue Roe were published, also scholarly studies by Ceridwen Lloyd-Morgan and Lisa Tickner, and an impressive bibliography by Cecily Langdale. By the beginning of this century, Mary Taubman was largely forgotten.

But she did publish a book in 1985. It was not the comprehensive volume that people had once expected, but an exquisite monograph that traces the development of Gwen John's simple designs into the monumental images of her late work, and examines the simultaneous detachment and intense personal involvement of her pictures, the close interweaving of self and subject.

The book is quite small in scale: an introductory essay of some 7,000 words with seventy-three picture plates (twenty-eight of them in colour), followed by twenty-nine pages of notes on the plates, a list of exhibitions and a chronology of events in Gwen John's life. But the book is written, arranged and presented with the 'detached and tender intensity' that Mary saw reflected in Gwen's work. That is the nature of its integrity.

Mary signed my copy of her book 'with love', thanking me in her preface for my 'unfailing help'. But it was an undeclared love we felt and in retrospect I sometimes feel my help did not go far enough. Biographers are at the mercy of their subjects, who may lead them all over the world before imprisoning them in their writing rooms. Beginning a life of Bernard Shaw, I went to live in Ireland in the mid-1970s. I left a few small Gwen John gouaches I had inherited with Mary while I was away, and she came once to visit me in Dublin. But inevitably we drifted apart with the sense of something un-begun, unfinished, and I was unable to help her much with the difficulties that arose between her and the John family.

In the early 1990s, when I came to prepare a new edition of my Augustus John biography, I contacted Mary and she sent me a marvellous letter describing her early research in France (it is now in the National Library of Wales).

I also went to see her once at her flat high up in Edinburgh, where she had begun painting again. We had supper together, drinking a glass of champagne as if in celebration. Later, when I was asked to give a talk at the Edinburgh Festival, I telephoned her, but she could not see me on the day I was to be there. One of her daughters came to my talk and afterwards she told me that Mary was suffering from dementia. The evening I telephoned she had dressed up in smart clothes and stood in her room with nowhere to go. When I heard this, and saw in my mind that solitary dressed-up figure, I was overcome with a sadness that seemed to have been dammed up for thirty years. And I thought of that tiny canvas of Gwen John's called *A Corner of the Artist's Room in Paris*, and of the precise and simple short passage in which Mary had described that room, the room Gwen herself called 'delicious':

> I can think of no other painting so powerful in its impact, so tender and intense, so imbued with the spirit of a portrait ... She came to regard her room as a refuge and a consolation indeed an extension of herself.

The room in that painting is empty, yet it is filled with Gwen's invisible presence and with the 'passionate melancholy' that Mary recognised as the hallmark of her work.

Recently I read an essay by Mary's lifelong friend Jane Miller, who visited her in the home in Scotland where she then lived. I take some comfort from her words: 'She [Mary] laughs and smiles a lot and I see none of that "lion face" that Alzheimer patients are famous for,' she writes. '... She is permanently fixed in the present ... Sometimes I think she may never have been happier.'

I like to think of her released from a past that was overshadowed by the tragic accidental death of her young son. And I hope she is also freed from a too-challenging future, which threatened to measure what she did against an ideal that was for ever unattainable. If she truly came to live in an undemanding present, then she may indeed have reached a place of calm. 'Calm's not life's crown,' Matthew Arnold wrote, 'though calm is well.'

Bottom Gear

When I first learnt to drive a car in the late 1960s I felt an enormous freedom. I could go anywhere, it seemed: I drove my car on to a train, a boat, even a plane, which flew me to France. Whatever the destination, wherever I landed, I was soon hurtling onwards. It was exhilarating.

All this whizzing gave me a sense of power – a modest power, because I had a modest car, a tiny DAF. But it became my friend. I could see it waiting for me from the window of my flat as I decided where we would go. I drove it for pleasure and also for work.

I had originally become interested in cars, I believe, because my father took such pride in them. Did I think the Ford Zodiacs, he asked me, were superior to the Ford Zephyrs? He had owned both and I felt wonderfully adult being asked such a question. Some colours, my father considered, helped cars to travel faster than others. I didn't understand this, but it somehow added to the magic of motoring and the sophistication of our conversation. My DAF was yellow and my father didn't think much of that. If you were going to have a colour, he advised me, make it red or blue.

My interest in cars increased as I got older and began writing biographies. My subjects' cars became magnified versions of themselves – at least they did when I wrote about them. Shaw, I realised, knew a great deal about the automobile; John knew nothing. And yet they both had about the same number of accidents and came through them miraculously uninjured. I must have picked up something from them – a cautionary rather than exemplary lesson – because I too have been uninjured even when a wasp got into my car and, taking both hands off the wheel to repel it, I careered into the car ahead of me.

The cars I had thirty or forty years ago would seem very simple and uninteresting to young people now. But I like simplicity, which is why I bought an automatic Honda Accord, which pretty well drove itself. I have driven Hondas now for so long that I am hoping the Honda Motor Company will soon sponsor me in some way.

In the first decade of this century I began to feel that the sense of freedom and the very magic of motoring were ebbing away. I have been told that this is because I am getting … less young. But I don't believe it. The fact is that there are fewer young men driving cars these days than there were when I was young – and those who do drive travel shorter distances.

All this is not simply my impression but the finding of a team of academics commissioned by the Centre for Transport Studies to make an 'in-depth analysis' of our motoring habits. They took their research up to 2007 but not beyond this, since everything from then onwards would be attributed to the recession. They found that company cars are being less used than in the last century and this puzzles the experts and worries some Members of Parliament. I believe that it can be attributed to the culture that led to our recession – a culture where money was not a means to an end but the end itself. If you make cuts in your company expenses then you have achieved an 'efficiency' that leads to greater profits and larger bonuses.

Equally puzzling apparently is the fact that there are more women drivers on the road today than there were a decade ago. Women have seldom been interested in cars, seeing them merely as a means of travelling from one place to another – which any serious motoring man will tell you is a very superficial view. My mother liked cars, but she preferred to be driven by a man than to drive herself – and so apparently did many women.

Automobiles used to be sold with girls in swimsuits stretched across the bonnets or walking invitingly with looks of intense desire round expensive sports cars. This of course was what we now see as a sexist gimmick designed to sell cars to men. It was almost as if you could get the girl with the car as a two-for-the-price-of-one bargain. 'Get a car: get the girl' was the caption. The reason that there are more women drivers now is that they have finally won a measure of independence. They prefer the freedom of driving to their own destinations.

Despite the larger number of women drivers, the average mileage we travel in cars has been decreasing. This 'is very strange and shocking', writes Richard Westcott, the BBC transport correspondent. He is a romantic of the road, overcome with memories of the past.

Today it is almost impossible to drive round London for five minutes without hearing the wail of police cars and ambulances. It is like being in a war. To drive less in such conditions seems to me common sense. The open road, which attracted early drivers, has given way to the rush-hour road, the road that is being dug up and presenting drivers with what appears to be a dangerous obstacle course. It is easier to take a train or a bus.

Driving in London resembles a long, agonisingly slow convoy of cars apparently in mourning for the dead, the vehicles full of red-faced, anguished drivers suffering from high blood pressure as they look for a legitimate parking place. Parking restrictions change dramatically from district to district, sometimes from one side of the road to the other. What is altering our driving habits is not just the increase in money but the decrease of pleasure.

The Congestion Charge zone in London has been blamed for much of what has been happening. Personally I welcomed it. Burglars refused to pay a fee to drive into it and the level of crime went down. But now that the zone has vanished again, they are back.

A Cat and Mouse Story

I grew up in a house that was crowded with dogs. Most of them belonged to my aunt, though a few of the less popular ones were passed on to my grandmother. As head of the household, my grandfather had to summon the vet from time to time, an excruciating business as he did not trust the telephone and, being unable to see whom he was speaking to, would raise his voice, making him sound very rude. Money was scarce and, if I was off colour, my grandfather would take the vet aside, offer him a glass of sherry (which he knew would not be accepted) and then ask him, man to man, about 'the boy' – which was me. Was there something we should get from Boots the Chemists to put colour back in my cheeks? My aunt got her novels from the library at Boots and could easily pick up some syrup or a tonic for the boy. When he did have to call on a doctor to see me, he would question him in a whisper about the dog's health.

Maybe it was because I felt these dogs were getting more attention than I was that I grew up preferring cats. I have never owned a cat – or any animal, come to that – but I will usually stop and have a few words with any I meet in the street or see wandering along garden walls. The places they perch amuse me – a ginger one down the road likes to sleep on the saddle of a motorbike.

My favourite cat was Zeus. Despite this godlike masculine name, Zeus was a small black female cat that belonged to my younger stepson Joe. When he and his family went away on holiday, Zeus would come to stay with my wife and me in the country. It did not seem to me an easy journey – lasting, by train and by car, four hours or so. I would worry a lot while Maggie was doing a lot, putting the purring Zeus into a travelling basket and dealing with any cat bureaucracy for the railways while I gave high-pitched whistles, which scholarly research had led me to believe Dr Johnson made to his cat, Hodge. We had a special game in the country, which involved Zeus leaping up and down the staircase as I shuttled a card along the bannister rails. The family archive reveals that she wrote some interesting postcards home, copying Maggie's and my handwriting and telling everyone that her main duty in the country was making sure the old couple were awake in time to see the sun rise every morning.

I particularly remember one lunch we had at Joe and Cath's house in London. Zeus liked playing with the children, Stanley and Connie, and after whizzing round the carpets and darting through our ankles she would stretch herself along the back of the sofa and gaze at the world outside. After her lunch she slept in the warm boiler room. But that day, I remember, she continued playing while we were eating, dashing from room to room in some mysterious cat game.

To add to the party, Maggie had brought some presents in a large canvas bag, which she left on the floor in the hall. We put the empty bag in the boot of the car before driving off in the late afternoon. It was Maggie who first became aware that we had a passenger. 'Did you hear that?' she asked. Eventually I did hear a small sound, but nothing I could recognise, nothing that showed up on the car's dashboard.

When we reached home and opened the boot we saw evidence that a mouse had been travelling with us and was settling down into the intestines of the car. Obviously it had been playing with Zeus, who had chased it into the bag. We brought it a small bowl of water and tried to come up with ways of rescuing it. I suggested that Maggie, who was between novels, might like to write a children's story featuring our mouse. She didn't find this particularly helpful.

A day or two later, still with the mouse on board, we drove to Cambridge where we were spending the weekend with a retired diplomat. The first evening one or two distinguished academics had been invited and I could not stop myself from telling the story of our mouse – though I think it was interpreted as a philosophical metaphor relating to Schrödinger's cat. Early next morning we saw the rather formal figure of our host, the ex-ambassador, striding secretly out to the car in his dressing gown with some delicacies for our mouse.

One day we realised that the mouse was no longer in the car. What had happened, where it had travelled, we never discovered. But the anxiety it provoked convinced me I had probably been wise never to take on the responsibility of a domestic animal.

PART TWO

Kipling and Mrs Ewing

Rudyard Kipling was born in Bombay at the end of 1865. Like many children whose parents lived and worked in India, he was sent 'home' at the age of six or seven to be properly educated in England. This was to be a most unhappy period of his life. He hardly saw his family and did not tell them of his loneliness and the bullying he suffered. It was not until 1936, the year before he died, that he wrote an autobiography, which made public the humiliation he had endured. *Something of Myself* was posthumously published the following year and criticised for containing very little of himself, the initial text having been severely edited under the guidance of his wife so as to omit any material that might be damaging.

But Kipling makes very clear his wretched time in England. For almost six years he lived at a house in the suburbs of Southsea, near Portsmouth. This establishment was under the supervision of a woman who took in children and introduced Kipling to what seemed the horrors of hell. 'I was regularly beaten,' he wrote. '... I have known a certain amount of bullying, but this was calculated torture ... it made me give attention to the lies I soon found it necessary to tell: and this, I presume, is the foundation of literary effort.' Reading was his single pleasure until 'deprivation from reading was added to my punishments'. At a 'terrible little day school' to which he was sent he became half blind and this was followed by a nervous breakdown.

But each December he entered paradise when he went to stay with his mother's sister, Aunt Georgy, whose house was full of love and affection. But he could not tell her, or anyone else, how he was being treated. It felt as if he were a 'moral leper'.

In 1878 he went to a school at the far end of England. 'My first year and a half was not pleasant,' he admitted. But he was fortunate in being physically some years in advance of his age and after fourteen he was no longer bullied. At last he began to enjoy school, to learn and made a friend of the headmaster. He was entering a new arena in which past enemies could be turned, not into friends exactly, but powerful allies. The fatal compromise of Liberalism, he later came to believe, led inevitably to bloodshed.

There was another world awaiting him. In the opening chapter of *Something of Myself*, Kipling refers to a novel called *Six to Sixteen* by Mrs Ewing. 'I owe more in circuitous ways to that tale than I can tell,' he wrote. Juliana Horatia Ewing had inherited her literary talent from her mother, the writer and editor Margaret Gatty, who soon saw that her daughter was to 'go far beyond me'. Juliana's demanding and sometimes tyrannical father, the Reverend Alfred Gatty, was not in favour of her marriage to Major Alexander Ewing. He worked in the British army's pay department, but the question was: how much did he get paid himself? The answer was too little – at least, that was what Juliana's father thought. But in *Six to Sixteen* his daughter strongly opposes the belief that 'money's the great thing in this world'. Though her father was not a bishop and her husband not a general, they provided Mrs Ewing with a modestly respectable place in society. Her trouble was ill health. She was unable eventually to travel abroad with her husband, and for the sake of the air and the water she went to Bath – where she died in her mid-forties.

Kipling did not tell readers of his autobiography the full title of Mrs Ewing's influential novel. *Six to Sixteen* had a surprising subtitle: *A Story for Girls*. So what, in its circuitous ways, did he owe this story for girls?

Mrs Ewing is usually described as a late-Victorian children's writer – she has a major entry in Daniel Hahn's new *Oxford Companion to Children's Literature*. But her *Story for Girls* is a novel for young adults. It is presented as an autobiography written by Margaret Vandaleur, whose early years, like those of Kipling's, were passed in India. 'The first six years of my life were spent chiefly with my Ayah,' she writes.

> I loved her very dearly. I kissed and fondled her dark cheeks as gladly as if they had been fair and ruddy, and oftener than I touched my mother's ... My most intimate friends were of the Ayah's complexion ... I have forgotten the language of my early childhood, but its tones had a familiar sound; those dark bright faces were like the faces of old friends, and my heart beat for a minute, as one is moved by some remembrance of an old home.

The story is told by an orphan, Margaret's parents having died from cholera and fever when their daughter was five or six. Kipling's parents had not died while he was that age, but it felt as if they were dead when they left him to the mortification of an English home and returned to India. Mrs Ewing describes the educational management of young girls in England during their 'awkward years' as being designed to make them 'feel stronger and happier'. She introduces us to the schoolmistress who is 'at once bland and solid', which seemed to produce 'a favourable impression on parents and guardians. Being stout, and between fifty and sixty years old, she was often described as "motherly".' But the children soon discovered that she was neither just nor truthful. She 'seemed to break promises, tell lies, open letters, pry into drawers and boxes, and listen at keyholes, from the highest sense of duty'. Though she prided herself on keeping the children 'under supervision', she never noticed that one of Margaret's school friends was seriously ill. 'I feel there has been culpable neglect,' she says mournfully when the doctor arrives to take the patient away to hospital. But the doctor corrects her. 'The illness sprang from the best motives,' he explains '... I have known too many cases in which ill results have been life-long and some in which they have been rapidly fatal.' In short, such schools were as harmful as prisons that let their inmates out into the world more dangerous than they had been when sent in.

What Kipling learnt from this fictional 'autobiography' was that English schools for girls were as unpleasant and dangerous as boys' schools. Mrs Ewing's stories for girls were the very opposite of Lord Chesterfield's letters to his son, written in the eighteenth century. They warned upper-class people against laughter because it occasioned 'a shocking distortion of the face'. Mrs Ewing, who had a natural sense of humour, intended her readers to laugh and it is very difficult not to do so when reading many of her pages.

In the novel a close friend of Margaret's tells her that certain vices such as cheating, lying, gluttony, petty gossip and malicious mischief-making were confined to the lower orders. But Margaret replies that she had learnt otherwise when she was a small child in India.

> I have heard polished gentleman lie, at a pinch, like the proverbial pickpocket, and pretty ladies fib as well as servant girls ... Customers cheat as much as shopkeepers, but I do think that many people who ought to 'know better' seem to forget that their honour as well as their interest is concerned in every bargain.

Rudyard Kipling had first read Mrs Ewing's novel when he was very young. Her early pages in India mirrored his own happiness at home there. He reread it during his school years in England, remembering it almost word for word over fifty years later when he was writing his autobiography. 'I knew it, as I know it still, almost by heart,' he wrote. 'Here was a history of real people and real things.' Mrs Ewing's novel helped him to survive when a schoolboy and may have come to his aid in later days of dejection. But after he returned to India and became a successful writer, he found himself in an 'unmeasurable gulf that lies between two races'.

By the time he won the Nobel Prize for Literature in 1907 he was well known as the private soldiers' poet and had gained fame for beating the drum on behalf of the British Empire. The British had indeed done some good work in India. They extended the

Indian railways and canals and established the first adequate forest service. Although the East India Company was there to trade and make a profit, it also reorganised the public works department, brought in civil servants and created a just legal system. The Company invested too in education, so that many Indians spoke excellent English and played enjoyable cricket (though no Englishman believed that an Indian eleven would ever get the better of the English team).

But none of this greatly appealed to Kipling – indeed he came to question it. While spreading their own version of culture through India, many of the British maintained a sense of superiority. There was a lack of generosity among them, an authoritarianism leading to acts of cruelty. 'An' if you treat a nigger to a dose of cleanin'-rod/'E's like to show you everything 'e owns,' wrote the young Kipling.

But, as he told the Irish writer John Stewart Collis later in his life, he did not believe that the British travelled abroad in order to create empires. On the contrary they simply travelled, as do all people who live on islands, to explore more of the world. Among them, he admitted, were some adventurous well-armed traders who arrived on the east coast of India. They found themselves in a land of warring tribes and soon observed that wherever the British travellers pitched their tents there was safety. You could go to bed without fear and wake up in peace. There was nothing more tranquil than a few guns. Eventually this handful of British voyagers spread their influence over the whole country and, to their surprise, the English found themselves in possession of a continent.

So what happened? What went wrong? Collis copied down what Kipling said and was to publish it in *An Irishman's England* (1937). Nothing need have gone wrong, Kipling had explained, if only a lot of busybodies had not insisted on 'democratising and elevating the people. They must be given a vote, they must be educated and all the rest of it ... And now we see the result.'

Kipling's circuitous journey from the heart of Mrs Ewing's novel to such a belief seems contrary to his international reputation as a great drum-beater for the empire. He was, as it were, two people. At different ages and in special circumstances he seemed to become his own opponent, challenging and suppressing in private what he sometimes wrote for the public and revealing what he put aside when addressing readers with his usual confidence.

Children's Books for Adults

In her life of Edith Nesbit, *A Woman of Passion,* Julia Briggs wrote that Nesbit's publisher was uncertain as to whether her books were aimed directly at children or at their parents, who could read to them aloud. I prefer the notion of children reading to their parents and reminding them of what childhood was like. But a more practical solution to this problem has recently come to me: Nesbit's most brilliant fiction, including *The Story of the Treasure Seekers* and *The Wouldbegoods,* together with other adventures of the Bastable family, are best read by adults in their second childhood.

The only Edith Nesbit story I read in my first childhood was *The Railway Children.* I thought it most exciting, but, reading the book now, I was a little disappointed. It seems to me the least original of her books and the most sentimental. There is less humour in it than in her Bastable books. The relationship between the children and the adults is rather weak and the plot repetitive, while the climax, which is surely obvious to most readers, takes all the characters by surprise. The story touches on contemporary political oppression at the beginning of a century that would lead to two world wars, but because this is beyond the understanding of the children (who believe that perfect justice belongs naturally to the adult world), nothing can be explained or explored. The most challenging element is what appears to be the book's invitation for children to play happily on railway tracks.

By contrast the Bastables' adventures are reconstructions of Nesbit's own intense experiences as a child with her two brothers and her sister. She recreates a world of magic and imagination near the frontier of an adult country where oddly straightforward chronology and mysterious business practices rule. She looks from one country into the other. This is the early autobiography of a novelist.

One of the books read by the Bastable children is *The Golden Age* by Kenneth Grahame. Nesbit admired, and was influenced by, Grahame's writing. Both of them use parody and allusion, and they had the ability to see events vividly through the eyes of children. Her stories are more hilarious – I have often had to put the book down laughing. His writing invents a more ideal fantasy.

When Nesbit wrote fairy tales about dangerous dragons, she had to invent an unusual winged hippogriff to steer the story to a happy ending. The fun lies in the very ordinary language in which she describes the most extreme and extraordinary happenings. Kenneth Grahame's reluctant dragon in *Dream Days,* his companion volume to *The Golden Age,* is not a monster from our nightmares but a dream creature of the most generous disposition. He has no wish to fight St George in case he might, by some unfortunate accident, hurt him. St George is obliged to challenge him because it is his business to fight dragons – and if he doesn't win the fight he might lose his sainthood. It is the people themselves who insist, despite all evidence to the contrary, that this dragon is their enemy. They need a fight (ideally to the death) to entertain them. Kenneth Grahame's amiable dragon has a similar role to that of the old nag Rocinante in Cervantes's *Don Quixote.* One story rewrites traditional fairy tales, the other ridicules tales of romantic chivalry.

This childlike satire on our adult behaviour is more strongly developed by the next generation of children's writers – particularly in the quintet of novels about the Borrowers, written for the most part during the 1950s by Mary Norton. These tiny people, who mimic what they sometimes call 'human beans', like to think of us giants as having been put on earth to manufacture useful small objects for them. There are, for example, safety pins (which become coat-hangers), cotton reels (on which to sit), stamps (which are placed as wonderful portraits and landscapes on their walls), toothbrushes (parts of which make excellent hairbrushes) and thimbles (from which they drink tea). All of these items and many more are borrowed or, as the giants would call it, 'stolen'.

We never see the Borrowers (or only very occasionally after drinking several glasses of fine Madeira). But we are aware of the number of objects that vanish all the time. Something is always missing and it is these disappearances that, despite their near invisibility, prove the existence of the Borrowers. It's elementary, my dear reader. As Sherlock Holmes explained: 'When you have eliminated the impossible, whatever remains, *however improbable*, must be the truth.'

These improbable beings have something in common with the inhabitants of the Island of Lilliput, where Gulliver was shipwrecked in the first part of Jonathan Swift's *Gulliver's Travels* (Mary Norton brings in the word 'shipwreck' to alert us to this connection). The Lilliputians were some six inches high (slightly taller, I calculate, than the Borrowers) and by recording their wars and social customs on such a diminished scale, Swift's satire made devastating ridicule of them – which is to say of us.

The three characters in Mary Norton's first book, *The Borrowers*, represent a recognisable human family. The head of the family is Pod, a most talented Borrower, able when young to 'walk the length of a laid dinner-table after the gong was rung, taking a nut or sweet from every dish, and down by a fold of the table-cloth as the first people came in at the door'. His wife Homily is an ingenious cook, very house-proud – but fearful of the world outside. Their daughter Arrietty, in her early teens, fears nothing – not even cats! She longs to explore 'the great out-doors', to bask in the sunlight, to run through the grass, swing on twigs like the birds: in short, to be free from the gloominess of her secret life under the floors and behind the wainscots of Firbank Hall, the great Georgian house where she lives with her parents. It is a hidden, safe existence, like the wartime lives of humans in towns and cities during the Second World War.

In 'the golden age', when this mansion was full of wealthy people and there was much to borrow, many little people lived there: the Rain-Barrels, the Linen-Presses and the Boot-Racks, the Brown Cupboard Boys, the rather superior Harpsichords and the Hon. John Studdingtons (who lived behind a portrait of John Studdington). Pod himself belonged to the Clock family, though Homily's mother was a mere Bell-Pull – which was why she was never invited to the Overmantels' parties. These aristocratic Overmantels were a stuck-up lot who lived in the wall high up behind the mantelpiece in the morning room where the human beans ate their first meal of the day. The Overmantel women were conceited, tweedy creatures who admired themselves in bits of the overmantel mirror; the men were serious whisky drinkers and tobacco-smokers. They lived on an eternal breakfast: 'toast and egg and snips of mushroom; sometimes sausage and crispy bacon with sips of tea and coffee'.

By the time *The Borrowers* begins, there is only one rich person and a couple of servants left in the house, and only the single Clock family of three small people. It follows that there is less to borrow, but also less chance of being seen. Nevertheless Arrietty has been seen by a nine-year-old boy and, to her parents' horror, makes friends with him. He brings the Clocks all sorts of terrific furniture from an old dolls' house in the attic; in payment for this Arrietty reads to him as he lies on his back in the garden, she standing on his shoulder, speaking into his ear and telling him when to turn the page. She improves his reading and at the same time educates herself, learning much about the mysterious world in which they all exist. But this coming together between giants and little people breaks the first rule of the Borrowers. There are good and bad people, artful and honest giants but, as Pod explains to Arrietty, they cannot be trusted: 'Steer clear of them – that's what I've always been told. No matter what they promise you. No good never really came to no one from any human being.'

And so it proves to be. The Boy's friendship accidentally leads to the Borrowers being seen by other humans who bring in a cat, a policeman and a rat-catcher carrying his vast equipment of poisons, snares and bellows with lethal gas – in addition to some terriers and a ferret. In the chaos, Pod, Homily and Arrietty escape to the great outdoors, its beauty and its danger, where they have many adventures *Afield*, *Afloat* and *Aloft*. Wherever they go, the same rules about humans apply. Though some are friendly, others seem frightened by such tiny travesties of themselves and wish to eliminate them, while a few try to capture them in order to make money. Such is the human condition. There is a reference in these adventures to Henry Fielding's mock-heroic farce *Tom Thumb*, who was sadly eaten by a cow, a *Tragedy of Tragedies* that brought tears of rare laughter to Jonathan Swift.

What reignites the ingenuity and humour of these volumes is the creation of a supreme Borrower of Borrowers, the amazing Spiller. He doesn't know how old he is and has no memory of his family beyond his mother telling him at breakfast: 'A dreadful spiller, that's what you are, aren't you?' So Dreadful Spiller he remains: an outdoors Borrower who, with his earth-dark face and bright black eyes, is a master of concealment, melting into the background, disappearing fast and becoming invisible. He is a miraculous hunter. He owns a couple of boats – an old wooden knife-box, which he cleverly guides along the river for long journeys carrying strange borrowed cargos, and the bottom half of an aluminium soap case, slightly dented, for more modest expeditions. He is fearless, but suddenly shy when saving the lives of the Clock family. His teasing smile greatly attracts Arrietty, for whom he embodies the whole wide out-of-doors world.

Spiller leads the Clocks to Homily's brother's family, which enables Mary Norton to balance self-independence against family life (so many people, so many rules, so much for show and so little for use). 'Poor Spiller,' thinks Arrietty. 'Solitary they called him … Perhaps that's what's the matter with me.' Mary Norton is not sentimental about families. She seems to prefer the individual enterprise of Spiller and Arrietty, who are both loners.

Four of Mary Norton's Borrowers' books were published within nine years. Then, after an interval of twenty-one years (and ten years before her death), she brought out her final volume, *The Borrowers Avenged*, in 1982. It begins where *The Borrowers Aloft* ended – as if no time has passed. Having made a complicated escape from an attic prison by balloon (an achievement overlooked by Richard Holmes in his book of balloons, *Falling Upwards*), the Clocks are led by Spiller on an adventurous journey to an ancient, overgrown rectory. Here, amid danger, excitement and surprise, they encounter new and old friends and enemies. One question remains: what will be the future for Arrietty? Will it be with Spiller, the Borrower who belongs to the outdoors, or with Peagreen, an attractive young Borrower with a charming smile, who was abandoned by the Overmantels and belongs to the indoor life? Perhaps this could be decided through a new literary prize written in competition by admiring borrowers of Mary Norton's characters.

Our Friends the Dead

On 15 July 1662 the Royal Society was founded and the sciences first securely planted in our civilisation. It was the beginning of the modern world: the dawning of the age of Newton. 'Nature and nature's laws lay hid in night./God said "Let Newton be!" And all was light.'

Not all poets were as welcoming as Alexander Pope. Coleridge, who believed that poetry was the antithesis to science, wrote that it would take 500 Newtons to go into the making of a Shakespeare or a Milton. And for William Blake, the image of Newton with his prism and his silent face was not of 'a mind forever voyaging through strange seas of thought, alone' (to use Wordsworth's description), but a mind limited by its single vision and a creature grounded by the weight of information technology.

Among the early Fellows elected to the Royal Society in the seventeenth century was John Aubrey, one of the most assiduously eccentric biographers in the language and author of *Brief Lives,* made up from spontaneous impressions that owed more to his imaginative gifts than to laborious research. Today he seems a surprising choice. But he shared with the younger scientists a great appetite for knowledge – though his imagination was medieval and he inhabited a strange twilight world. He was a dealer in odds and ends, a seeker after apparitions, impulses, marvels, magic. It was not beyond him, in the interests of statistical scholarship, to pursue second-sighted persons in Scotland, or make an inventory of 'corps candles' in Wales. He liked to dissect prophecies, record the glances of love and envy, note the malodorous twangs left by departing ghosts. He was an unlucky advocate, a profound astrologer, dangerous alchemist and an eventful bankrupt. His business affairs 'ran kim kam: nothing took effect'. But he was never happy, he declared, until he had lost everything.

One of his contemporaries described him as 'a shiftless person, roving and magotieheaded, and sometimes little better than crazed'. And yet his friends still loved and valued him for what they called his 'most ingeniose conversation'. And it was this ingeniose conversation that we can still hear in his *Brief Lives.* His dream lay in what he described as 'the retrieving of those Forgotten Things from oblivion [which] in some sort resembles the Art of the Conjuror, which make those walk and appear that have layen on the grave many years; and to represent as it were to the eie, the places, Customs and Fashions that were Old Times'.

Aubrey was an amateur, both in the sense of being unprofessional and of writing for the love of the thing – out of passionate curiosity about human nature and the need for knowledge. *Brief Lives* was not published until more than a hundred years after his death – he died in 1697 and *Brief Lives* came out in 1813. The 'fragments of a shipwreck' that he left have been made into a seaworthy vessel by several modern editors, and the book is still in print today. Indeed, it has been dramatised for the radio, put on the stage, even filmed. But why? After all, Aubrey merely provides exotic glimpses into an obsolete world. He belongs to that night which Newton's coming had banished. So what is his enduring quality?

Of course, he has charm. But then, what is charm? Is it a literary virtue? Is it even a condition of virtue? In biography, I would suggest, charm is often a form of Keats's 'negative capability'. Modern biographers are cursed by an 'irritable reaching after fact and reason'. But they also, the best of them, 'pick about the gravel' with their subjects to attain an intense involvement with them, a preoccupation. This is certainly what John Aubrey did. Crazed and magotieheaded he might be, with one foot in the world of scientific fact, and one foot in the surreal world of superstition and fantasy, but he is a symbolic figure in modern biography. In a sense he is our Laurence Sterne, and *Brief Lives* our *Tristram Shandy*. Both works are crack-brained, half-crazy essays on the human mind, using humour as a device for peculiar insight. Aubrey was simultaneously behind the times and ahead of them: a time traveller, as it were, as we are.

Most critics would agree that modern biography did not begin until half a century after Aubrey's death. Some would date it to 1744, when Samuel Johnson's *Life of Mr Richard Savage* was published; others to Monday, 16 May 1763, the day that the 22-year-old James Boswell first met Dr Johnson, then in his fifty-fourth year, at a London bookshop; and others would choose 1791, when Boswell's *Life of Samuel Johnson* finally appeared. Whatever date you choose, Boswell and Johnson are recognised as the two father figures of modern biography. Johnson remarked to Boswell during their tour of the Hebrides that he 'did not know any literary man's life in England well-written'. This they both changed.

What is common to Johnson's *Life of Savage* and Boswell's *Life of Johnson* is the strong autobiographical ingredient. Johnson said that 'nobody can write the life of a man, but those who have eat and drunk and lived in social intercourse with him'. Though dressed up in some fine objective clothing and the paraphernalia of research, both books are nakedly subjective works. Johnson really comes alive in Boswell's biography only when Boswell appears on the page. For Boswell was the writer of what Johnson called a 'very pretty journal' – and most of his journals, like Aubrey's *Lives*, were published posthumously.

It is clear that people only became real to Boswell when he could actually see and hear them: in short, when he could enter their world. Or are they entering his world? Boswell's *Life of Johnson* is in some respects the first draft of Boswell's autobiography. Some say that Boswell resurrected Johnson; others that Johnson lies imprisoned in Boswell's book. How Boswell posthumously possessed Johnson and, like a great theatrical director, produced him for an audience of readers as a tremendous John Bull character, almost Dickensian in his exaggerated performance, was brilliantly indicated by an anthology called *Johnson Without Boswell*, put together by the critic Hugh Kingsmill. This was followed, over the next forty years, by several biographies of Johnson, which tried to rescue him and give him new, independent life, but, to the indignation of Johnsonian scholars, readers kept going back to Boswell.

In our own time, the biographer Richard Holmes has ingeniously shown how Johnson recreated the life of Savage as if it were his own buried life; a haunting, violent, dark life of the imagination that might have had as its epigraph: 'There but for the grace of God go I.' Holmes's *Dr Johnson & Mr Savage* presents us with a version of R. L. Stevenson's *Dr Jekyll and Mr Hyde*. Between the lines of Johnson's romantic account of Savage's early life, Holmes (our modern detective) reveals how the author identified with his subject. Here was his alternative life, the life he had never lived – but which festered in his imagination. We could never have guessed any of this from the pages of Boswell's biography because Boswell was attempting his own imaginative recreation, continually exhorting himself to 'think of Johnson', 'remember Johnson' and even 'be Johnson'. He did not actually imitate Johnson, but 'invented' him (to use Bernard Shaw's word) in the image of someone he would like to be. The world became a great court in which Johnson, its supreme barrister, scores fantastical victories over other men – that was the dream of the unsuccessful lawyer Boswell.

But, beyond Boswell's world, Richard Holmes shows Johnson growing fascinated by Savage's criminal career. He seems strangely sympathetic to it, even tempted by it. As they walked together at night, Johnson was following a parallel course to that of his dangerous friend – which, metaphorically, is what all biographers do – including Boswell. 'It appears to me that mine is the best plan for biography that can be conceived,' Boswell wrote, 'for my readers will, as near as may be, accompany Johnson in this progress, and as it were see each scene as it happened.'

Unlike Boswell, Johnson makes himself largely invisible as he patrols the streets of London with Savage by night. Then, more than 250 years later, Richard Holmes goes on these same walks through London: he takes Johnson's place. He is another time traveller, like Aubrey, seeking intimacy with the past. And, being

Holmes, he is studying the ground for clues to a deeper understanding. He discovers that Johnson suppresses damning evidence
against his friend, that he is subject to Savage's insidious charm: it
is essentially the same criticism that a few avid Wordsworthians
bring against Holmes's *Life of Coleridge*. So we come to that word
again: charm. Richard Holmes understands charm. He possesses
it. He is a miraculously seductive writer. He persuades us that
biography has some of the imaginative qualities of fiction – its
immediacy and mythic qualities. In his pages, Savage becomes an
urbane Mephistopheles, and Johnson a youthful Faust.

Between the age of Johnson and Boswell, and the beginning of
Queen Victoria's reign, the story of biography can be followed
through two remarkable books. The first is William Godwin's life
of Mary Wollstonecraft, published in 1798 with the title *Memoirs
of the Author of a Vindication of the Rights of Woman*: the second,
William Hazlitt's *Liber Amoris or The New Pygmalion,* published
in 1823.

The two books may appear to have little in common. Godwin's
biography of his wife, who had recently died following the birth
of their only child, is a determined attempt to provide an authentic narrative of the life and career of a woman whose intelligence,
unlike his own, was largely intuitive. Hazlitt's account of his
painful infatuation with his landlady's daughter, Sarah Walker,
is a cry of anguish sustained through several transcriptions and
some all-too-lightly edited letters to friends. The book makes
little pretence at reaching objectivity.

What both books have in common is grief, the passion of grief,
out of which, in their very different ways, they have been struck.
Godwin's grief moves him to do what he believes his wife would
most have wanted: to publish a vindication of her rights. In a
sense, he is carrying on her work by recreating the scenes and
incidents, passions and mortifications that sprang from her ardent
nature – including the 'species of connection for which her heart
secretly panted'. With extraordinary fairness, he tells us of her
romantic inclinations towards Henry Fuseli, her sexual enthral-
ment to Gilbert Imlay and the birth of their illegitimate child. He
owes this to her memory, he believes, and 'in the judgement of

honour and reason' he deliberately flies in the face of 'prudence or delicacy' and the 'factitious rules of decorum', passing on to his readers, for example, the knowledge that 'during her whole illness not one word of religious cast fell from her lips'.

'Love, dear, delusive love' – Mary Wollstonecraft's explanation of her unwise attachment to Gilbert Imlay – reverberates through the pages of *Liber Amoris*. 'I was in the dupe of friendship and the cool of love,' Hazlitt confessed. '... I cannot forget her, and I can find no other like what she seemed.' She seemed an angel, a saint, but is transformed into a witch, a little vixen, as idealistic love gives way to disillusion and jealousy. It is the tragedy of Othello played out in a lodging house and made no less tragic by the mercenary and uninteresting nature of the beautiful Sarah Walker.

The book is not well crafted. We are simply given what amounts to the raw materials for a book that Hazlitt was unable to write. 'I sit and indulge my grief by the hour ... Would I had never seen her.' *Liber Amoris* was advertised as being transcribed by 'a native of North Britain' shortly before he 'set out for the Continent in hopes of benefiting by a change of scene'. But he died, we are told, soon afterwards in the Netherlands – 'it is supposed of disappointment preying on a sickly frame and morbid state of mind'. But this fictitious death deceived no one – yet it signified what was for Hazlitt an emotional truth. 'She was my life,' he wrote. '... I am now inclosed [*sic*] in a dungeon of despair ... nature is dead around me.' Like Godwin's biography, Hazlitt's memoir did not attempt to spare his readers the embarrassments of his state of mind. He made their inclusion a point of honour – a 'pledge that was held sacred' to the dead author.

'A philosophical serpent ... [a] joyous hyena in petticoats,' was Horace Walpole's description of Mary Wollstonecraft, while Coleridge dismissed Hazlitt as 'singularly repulsive'. Such verdicts helped to bury the reputations of both writers until their renaissance in the twentieth century. Godwin's and Hazlitt's books were lost in the dark age of Victorianism. Nineteenth-century biographers lost the art of reversing the flow of time and judged their subjects by Victorian values. They regarded Boswell as a vulgar and ridiculous Sancho Panza, a small burlesque figure for ever fixed in their minds by Macaulay's eloquently damning description of him as 'servile and impertinent, shallow and pedantic, and a sot, bloated with family pride, and eternally blustering ... always laying himself at the feet of some eminent man, and begging to be spat upon and trampled upon'. In Macaulay's opinion, which was extraordinarily influential with the Victorians, Boswell appears to have written a masterpiece by accident – on the same principle that a monkey, one among several millions, might hit upon the keys and produce a play by Shakespeare. Macaulay was far more frequently quoted than Wordsworth, who praised Boswell's life of Johnson for breaking taboos, tearing down the partition between public and private life, and giving the readers intimate details of his dead friend.

The Victorian age rebuilt those partitions and re-established those taboos. They hemmed you in: you could no longer travel though time, no longer tell the truth. In his final book, *My Relations with Carlyle* (written in 1887 and published posthumously in 1903), James Anthony Froude explained the impossibility of writing a truthful life of Thomas Carlyle in his two volume biography (1882). Writing a nineteenth-century life resembled the dire mechanical occupation of which Blake accused Newton. Public career plus private sentimentality in the background seems to have been the formula. What biography needed was a Hubble telescope – an extraordinary eye to penetrate human nature. For more than a century Boswell was, in the words of Macaulay (a man of great parliamentary invective), the nonpareil of biographers.

From this solemn era we were rescued by two far-seeing books: an absorbing autobiography and a devastating quartet of biographical essays. Edmund Gosse's *Father and Son* went back to the struggle between science and religion. The father, Philip Gosse, was a Fellow of the Royal Society, his son, a Fellow Royal Society of Literature. Within their relationship, and through the agonised struggles of the father to reconcile the Book of Genesis with his knowledge of geology, we see the ferment erupting over the post-Darwinian world. It is a book that humanises our evolutionary history and ushers the confessional autobiography into twentieth-century literature.

'Human beings are too important to be treated as mere symptoms of the past,' wrote Lytton Strachey in his preface to *Eminent Victorians*. 'They have a value which is eternal and must be felt for its own sake.' Strachey's preface, which distanced biography from conventional history, was to act as a manifesto for modern biographers; and the book itself revealed an attack on his parents' generation: on its materialism at home and imperialism abroad, its backward-looking education system, its suspect evangelism, even its neurotic humanitarianism: all done in four acerbic miniatures – on Cardinal Manning, Florence Nightingale, Dr Arnold and General Gordon of Khartoum.

Strachey's achievement was to release biography from its hagiographical past, from the public life-and-letters format practised by the Victorians. He was to use the romantic novel as a model for his life of Queen Victoria, and then an ancient-and-modern combination of Elizabethan melodrama and Freudian analysis for his tragic history of *Elizabeth and Essex*. He also smuggled sexual deviancy into British history and culture under cover of his highly readable style. Some critics believed he led not only to debunking but also to pastiche and 'faction', with its speculations spilling into invention. Certainly the late twentieth century was a time for experiment – from the imaginary conversations in Peter Ackroyd's *Dickens* to the recorded interviews of Humphrey Carpenter's *Robert Runcie*.

It is surprising how widely British biography travelled during the twentieth century. If you find yourself reading a life of Strindberg or Ibsen, Tolstoy or Chekhov, Thomas Mann, Matisse, Sartre, Picasso or Primo Levi you may well be reading a book by a British biographer. We were inclined to relish our amateur status, unlike most American biographers, who are generally to be found in universities. George Eliot's biographer, Kathryn Hughes, has argued that it would be beneficial to end biography's intellectual isolation. This is the thinking behind the MA course on 'life-writing' at the University of Buckingham, which was founded in 1996 by Disraeli's biographer Jane Ridley, and also the one founded in 2001 at the University of East Anglia, where both Kathryn Hughes and Richard Holmes have taught.

Twentieth-century biographical innovations from A. J. A. Symons's famous *Quest for Corvo* in 1934 to Ian Hamilton's *In Search of J. D. Salinger*, a miraculous feat of making bricks without straw, first published in 1988, moved literary biographies towards imaginative thrillers written with the skill of novelists. So began a range of imaginative non-fiction writing that developed from orthodox biography – books such as Geoff Dyer's *Out of Sheer Rage*, a vivid account of not writing the life of D. H. Lawrence, and Julia Blackburn's surreal meditation *Daisy Bates in the Desert*, which grew from her subject's fantasies.

But a life of James Joyce published in 1959 (and revised in 1982) raised the quality of literary biography and stimulated later biographers such as Richard Holmes. This was written by Richard Ellmann, an American academic who was to specialise in Irish subjects – Yeats and Wilde – as well as his celebrated life of Joyce. But although these literary biographers stimulated other writers, it distanced biography from serious literature. Students are told that the life of a writer has on the whole little or no connection with what he or she wrote. Fictional literature moves with the times and eventually belongs to the reader, who is guided by the professional academic.

Essays on the novel and plays seldom refer these days to literary biographies – and literature is often focused solely on fiction. I do not see novelists and biographers as enemies. They belong to the same family. What seems strange is that, as life-writing is no longer seen as part of literature, the number of first-rate biographers has increased. Asked by a newspaper to name twenty women biographers, I did so without difficulty (and I could have added two or three more). But what is difficult, indeed impossible, is to choose one that stands out above the rest. As for this essay, I can choose one of the best living biographers only aesthetically by linking her to the beginning of this essay. That is Ruth Scurr, who wrote the life of Aubrey that was published in 2015. She is no less a pioneer than Aubrey himself.

What's in a Name?

At the end of an essay published in the *Slightly Foxed Quarterly* in the spring of 2009, Jennie Erdal describes herself as 'an editor and translator' who 'has written over a dozen books, but is the author of only one of them – *Ghosting: A Double Life,* a memoir that attempts to explain why'. This memoir is mainly focused on the semi-fictional career she created for her publisher-employer. The paperback cover has the picture of a girl's face, her eyes open as if awakening from a dream. But it is 'someone else's dream'.

The book opens with a love letter she has drafted to be copied 'onto embossed notepaper' and signed 'with a flourish' by her employer, who sends it to his wife. But there is something odd about this love letter. Jennie Erdal is a careful writer – so why is she so unconvincing?

As I read further into *Ghosting* I found an answer. A few years after she had begun working for this publisher, her husband Graham, a Shakespeare scholar, had travelled to Australia for two months on an academic fellowship. 'We weren't very good at being apart,' she writes. 'Up till then we had been separated for only a day or two at a time.' Their three children (aged nine, seven and five) were 'madly excited' that their father was coming home. Only he wasn't coming home; he was simply returning to the airport, where he could tell his wife that 'they were to be apart for ever'. He had fallen in love with a girl in Australia. This was astonishing since, vowing never to be parted again, they had been writing 'long, loving, missing-you letters … I have them still'. So much for men's love letters!

In her early years Jennie had been anxious to discover the purpose and meaning of life. But her parents had no interest in such stuff. Her father was a market gardener and she was closest to him when they shared the intimacy of skinning rabbits. Her mother had shown academic promise when young but left school to look after her dying mother. Feeling that she had been denied a better life, she began to sell Spirella corsets from her bedroom and with the money was able to send her daughter to have elocution lessons. This, she believed, would give her access to a higher social status where they lived in Scotland. What Jennie learnt was that ordinary men and women can be as eccentric as extraordinary people. This became useful information when she was seduced (the word is hers) by her eccentric publisher.

At university she had learnt the Russian language and studied Russian literature, to which she was to add other languages – French, German and Spanish – as well as deepening her knowledge of English literature. By 1980 she had begun translating the memoirs of Leonid Pasternak, the artist-father of the poet and novelist Boris Pasternak. She sent a chapter to Quartet, the most 'radical and risk-taking' of all the publishers in London – and they accepted it. So began her career as a translator.

In 1981 she travelled down from Scotland to meet her publisher. At his penthouse overlooking Soho she saw on the walls his pictures of half-naked women and enormous cats. 'Setting the wall ablaze' was a huge tiger skin with black and orange stripes. She decided to call him Tiger and, kissing her hand, he told her he liked the name. His actual name does not appear in the narrative of *Ghosting*. Nor does her own family name, which is why I am calling her Jennie.

Tiger drove her in his Rolls-Royce to Oxford, where she could introduce him to Leonid Pasternak's daughter Josephine. He wanted to meet her in order to buy some of her father's pictures. Jennie had already told him there was no chance of the family selling these pictures. On their journey she repeated that Josephine was absolutely resolute over this. But Tiger was equally resolute. 'You don't understand,' he told her. '*I have to have them ...* She'll sell them to me.' 'She won't,' Jennie insisted. But she did. He charmed her, almost hypnotised her. As Jennie was to discover, he made a habit of getting what he wanted. All the girls in his office 'loved to please him'.

To thank Jennie for enabling this sale, Tiger offered her an immediate job with a salary of £5,000 per year (approximately equivalent to £20,000 today) with all expenses paid. As a 'commissioning editor' she would work at home in Scotland, travelling to London for editorial meetings and accompanying Tiger to the yearly Frankfurt Book Fairs. One thing was obvious: she could earn more from being a publisher than a translator. And she was both: a translator and an independent editor in charge of a successful list of Russian publications. Her own first two translations – *The Memoirs of Leonid Pasternak* (1982) and Leonid Borodin's *The Year of Miracle and Grief* (1984) both have her married name on the jackets: Jennifer Bradshaw (another name not mentioned in *Ghosting*). This was a perfect job – until Graham Bradshaw left her.

On her next visit to London she told Tiger what had happened. 'I was moved by his gentleness and compassion,' she remembered. He assured her that her job was safe and her income would be increased. She became his 'personal assistant' and for the next fifteen years would work in close collaboration with him. He soon came up with one of his brilliant ideas on which they would work together: interviews with remarkable women – fifty or a hundred of them, or why not two, three or four hundred? It would be a bestseller and she would have half the royalties. There was so much work that she had no time to think of her missing husband. Her job was to gather the initial research and provide Tiger with some questions for his two-hour discussions with almost 400 women in Europe and America. He would send his transcripts to Scotland, where she reduced some 3 million words to approximately 600,000 words, shaping the text into various subtitles: Early Influences, Feminism, Relationships, Sexuality, etc. Any free time left to her she used for writing a 'historical account of the treatment of women in literature and mythology'. The book, almost 1,200 pages long, was published in 1987 with the simple title *Women*. And Tiger was 'in heaven'.

Jennie's work on the book had left her ill with exhaustion but earning an immediate bonus of £8,500 (approximately £22,000 today). This was the beginning of several interview collections, published over the next dozen years, in which Tiger appears as the author. 'When he was pleased, I too was pleased,' Jennie wrote. '…We made a great team, the author often said. And we did.'

Jennie was soon writing newspaper articles, reviews and speeches under Tiger's name. It was not a unique arrangement. There are people who write the queen's words, the prime minister's speeches and other public orations to save important people time – and lend them syntax. Jennie was providing what Tiger coveted: a new self. She became a different sort of translator – someone who understood his empty pages and filled them with the words he needed. Sometimes she added her own ideas, as if the two of them were almost the same person.

Their arrangements soon grew more ambitious. Tiger was delighted with their volumes of interviews, but they were all 'non-fiction' – which sounded rather negative. Something should be done about this. He was a grown-up man who had not yet grown up. He lived in the future – a landscape that was always changing. He needed now to become a novelist as well as a character within his novel. Like a magical typist, Jennie could write the necessary sentences. It would be their closest partnership.

He told her how important it was to have a beautiful jacket. And the plot must also be beautiful. A married man falls in love with a girl. There is huge passion between them and much distinguished sex. To put this on paper should not take long. The best place to create romance was, of course, France. He would take her to a place he owned in the Dordogne. She had been there before to help him avoid the horror of being alone. Unfortunately solitude was what she needed for writing. It was not easy.

But 1994 was a good year. She had overcome the depression following her divorce. And there was still love in her life: love for her three children and their love for her. There was also this strange love of words gathering round her while she worked for Tiger. Recently, adult love too was coming back into her life with a man called David Erdal – another name that finds no place in *Ghosting*.

To begin Tiger's novel she read a mass of contemporary fiction, examining the structures and techniques. She could not help inserting bits and pieces from her own life. But bringing Tiger's boyish fantasies and her literary aspirations together was a challenge. *A Timeless Passion* took shape, slowly in his view, quickly in hers, and it was published in 1995.

Tiger immediately began mapping out their second work of fiction. A single novel, he explained, was too lonely – almost an accident. He wanted to break new ground. When the man had sex with one of two women in the story both women would have an orgasm even though one of them was on the other side of the world. It was as if they shared a single body.

This hardly bore thinking about. Yet Jennie 'thought about it constantly'. She inserted episodes from her own life, including a caricature of her former husband, the man she had once loved but who became someone who loved himself – a case of painful self-adulation. She invented other memories for her Tiger-like hero, hoping he would be happy with them. But he was disappointed by *Tara and Claire*.

He soon cheered up. It was surprising how seriously an opinionated man like Tiger valued reviews. He read out loud one by the novelist Alice Thomas Ellis. She praised him for having 'a sensitivity and an insight into human nature unusual in a man, and he writes quite beautifully'.

Nevertheless it was obvious to Tiger that they must give birth to his third novel, one in which they introduced God as a minor character. But something was changing in Jennie's life.

She continued impersonating Tiger, writing his erotic articles and pen portraits of women in newspapers and magazines. 'We were like two trapeze artists performing dangerous stunts in mid-air,' she wrote. Freeing herself from his fiction, she was thinking of writing a novel of her own. 'Whenever I managed to shake off the shackles of the ghost, I quite enjoyed writing,' she wrote. '... [It] has a lot to do with unlocking secrets that are inside you.'

Ghosting was a strange book with which to 'shake off the shackles off the ghost'. It conceals as many secrets as it reveals. She did not tell readers her family name in her autobiographical chapters or her first husband's surname, which she used as a writer until 1996 (it was Jennifer Bradshaw who also appeared on the jackets of her early Russian translations). Another secret is her marriage that year – when she becomes Jennie Erdal. In *Ghosting* she refers to this second husband as N-H (new husband). Eight years later, he appears merely as 'the man at home' in the acknowledgements of her novel *The Missing Shade of Blue.*

She left Quartet at a period of its financial difficulty and after her husband complained that Tiger had become 'too big in your life'. It was not easy. But 'the dishonesty was beginning to weigh more heavily', she wrote. '… I considered my mental state, my bank balance, my home life, my blood pressure.'

Ghosting became a bestseller and was translated into several languages. Tiger appears as quixotic, vainglorious, dictatorial and belligerent, with a childlike fear of solitude. But he is also generous, amusing, hard-working, charming and wholly loveable.

What she had minded was the praise that year after year passed by her and focused on him. Reviewing *Women* in 1987, the *Daily Telegraph* critic made the point that 'it has taken a man to write the most revealing book about woman'. In *Ghosting* she wrote of her resolution 'to pull out of this bizarre arrangement. To give up the ghost.' It had become an autobiography that involved not one but two men.

The way to get rid of her deepening worries was to rewrite the past and eliminate her sense of injustice. It seemed at times that she had not existed. People would ask her if she had read any of Tiger's books – she who had written them! Reading this in *Ghosting* in 2004 I thought that Tiger had gone unnecessarily far in keeping her so invisible.

But looking again at the opening pages of *Women,* I find that Tiger has praised someone who 'organised the historical background research, oversaw the transcription and typing of the taped interviews, edited the transcripts and finally collated the vast quantity of material that goes to make up the bulk of the book. Her task has been the most daunting of all, since time was of the essence from the start.' There are similar acknowledgements in the other interview books, as well as the first of their novels. Both

Women and *A Timeless Passion* are dedicated to Tiger's wife Maria and there is a special acknowledgement to the same 'invaluable' editor. These tributes were for Jennifer Bradshaw, a name that meant nothing to readers of *Ghosting*. But Jennifer Bradshaw was well known at Quartet as a translator and senior editor. The only people left ignorant were Jennie Erdal's readers. Only in their second novel, *Tara and Claire*, published after her marriage, could Tiger pay tribute to Jennie Erdal for her 'immense' contribution.

The name 'Tiger' did not conceal the identity of the well-known proprietor of Quartet Books. Indeed, when a page of copyright acknowledgements was added at the end of *Ghosting*, Naim Attallah's name appeared half-a-dozen times. The reviewers wrote openly of him, often making fun of him. The text had been sent to him and a paragraph at the beginning of the book thanks 'Tiger, who inspired this story and allowed it to be told'.

The final two pages of *Ghosting* shows their loving farewell. 'He lived as people rarely do nowadays, dangerously and passionately,' Jennie Erdal wrote. '... In an age of big business publishing characterised by remoteness and detachment, he was heroically original and human ... Accountants moved in, but there was no dramatic Fall of Empire ... Tiger rose from the ashes, wearing his brightest colours and finest jewels ... I left the palace bearing a gift of a Mont Blanc pen ... we hugged each other ... I caught a No. 12 bus and tears fell all the way to Waterloo.' At the end of her journey, back in Scotland, she began writing her book.

In the third volume of his autobiography, *Fulfilment & Betrayal 1975–1995*, which was published in 2007, Naim Attallah gave his response. He could not understand why she had written *Ghosting* and destroyed the memory of their attachment – 'a memory I would have treasured for the rest of my life'. What hurt him most was the way she had dealt with the closest of their collaborations: their two novels. The themes had been his. He would ring her each day, often several times a day, to speak about these books and suggest changes when she sent him each chapter. But 'I would never dispute the fact that the finished books were realised through her writing'. They had made 'a vow' and she had broken it. He pulped all the unsold copies of their novels and omitted the titles from the list of literary works in his other books (though not in *Who's Who*). It was 'heartbreaking'.

Ghosting had been written about him but not for him. She dedicated it to her husband.

For N-H
without whom

Without him it would never have been written.

A Hook in the Heart

Violet Trefusis, who wrote her novels either in French or English, was essentially a European writer. She travelled widely throughout her life and liked to explore, partly as comedy, partly as a stimulant to tragedy, the cultural differences between European countries. In *The Hook in the Heart,* written in English and begun during the mid-to-late 1920s, when she was in her early thirties, she contrasts France, where she was happiest as an adult, with Spain. She had visited Spain and makes some acute observations of its people and impressions of its landscape. But she places a fantasy at the core of this social realism and guides her readers into a fairyland castle. Here they find the servants all asleep, encounter a Machiavellian devil disguised as a priest and witness a matriarchal figure tempting our heroine with an ill-omened necklace. This is a magical place of dreams and nightmares.

To Cécile, the central character in the novel, France (and especially Paris) had been a place of conventions and compromises, a sophisticated community that belonged to women as much as to men. But, having been turned down by an attractive Frenchman, she decides to put the flirtations and playacting of French society behind her and become engaged to a punctilious Spanish duke. She is also ready to leave her mother, whose chief passion is a horror of scandal (which may bring to mind Violet Trefusis's mother, Alice Keppel, a royal mistress of extreme discretion). Cécile's mother has done little to support her daughter. But on the night before her wedding, she offers some advice. 'The Spaniards are very different from the French – more – more strict – and less – conciliatory,' she explains. Cécile must take care not to vex her husband, she adds, and to treat his revered grandmother, the dowager duchess, with polite formality.

Mothers do not come out well in this novel. Cécile's husband Alfonzo, Duke of Cantijo, has a plump and sparkling widow as his mother. She is full of risky stories orchestrated by shrill bursts of laughter and lives solely for society. In short she is 'futile almost beyond the range of ill nature'.

What these two mothers lack is love, and lacking love they have none to give their children who, in turn, are marrying without love. This is what troubles Cécile in the opening paragraph of the novel. But Alfonzo is untroubled. He is presented as a typical Spanish aristocrat: decent, loyal and unimaginative, with a proud simplicity of character and narrow ambitions. He is marrying from duty and in the belief (suggested to him by an enlightened aunt) that a well-born, Catholic Frenchwoman will bring lightness into his morose family.

But Alfonzo is burdened by two disadvantages. Having been educated at Oxford he has become tainted by English culture: its demands of reticence and a consuming passion for sport that leave little space for anything else. He lives under the terrible shadow of his grandmother, the dowager duchess, a dark figure shrouded in widow's weeds. She is presented as an embodiment of impenitence (hidden under a cloak of high principles) who has already brought about one tragedy in the castle before the novel begins. Now she plots a devious strategy to rob Cécile of her self-esteem. The source of her bitterness, we discover, lies in having been humiliated by her late husband. Now loveless, she suffers without knowing it from boredom, filling the emptiness with thoughts of revenge and the pursuit of power. The need for sexual love, the search, possession and loss of it, permeate this novel.

After several weeks of married life Cécile finds it hard to believe that sex 'is what makes people torture themselves, fight each other'. It has been an unemotional nightly business between her and Alfonzo. But instinctively she knows what is missing. She might have learnt to do without passionate love in France, but Spain seems to provoke what it forbids. Trefusis gives us a vivid description of Cécile's erotic excitement while watching the gypsy dancers at Seville: 'All her body is crying out for the invisible lover whom she alone can see.' What she has seen in the streets are lovers with their faces pressed together, but separated by window grills and bars. The customs of the country keep them apart.

Determined not to be imprisoned by such restrictions, she takes herself out of her husband's castle for ever-lengthening walks alone. This independence shocks Alfonzo and his family – and even alarms the servants. Women in Spain, she is told, do not get up in the morning; they lie in bed, write letters, read books, miss appointments and live according to the rhythm of Spanish life, where no one hurries, meals are served at impossible hours, and time itself is abolished. But Cécile is impatient. She wants to go everywhere and see everything. Her walks become more adventurous. 'I never realised how much I loved solitude,' she innocently writes in a letter to Alfonzo's Aunt Luz, who becomes her secret ally. She cannot admit to herself that what she really wants is to make her invisible lover a physical reality. When she meets a young gypsy dancer with a natural sense of intimacy and the odour of a wild animal, she is immediately caught in his spell. They eat cherries together under a fruit tree that is Trefusis's equivalent of the Tree of the Knowledge of Good and Evil. Then the drama of the novel begins. Is sorrow better than safety? Is grief preferable to boredom? These are the questions she must answer.

Shortly after the First World War, when Violet Trefusis had begun experimenting with novels, she complained that she had little confidence in herself as a writer. 'My limitations are becoming more and more apparent ... I can only see my side of the question; I am blind to the other person's.' But by the late 1920s she was overcoming this limitation by making her characters embody part of the culture in which they live. Alfonzo and the amoral gypsy Kalo both live in Spain, but the duke and the gypsy represent opposing social cultures that give dramatic tension to the story.

There are several similarities in *The Hook in the Heart* to Trefusis's other novels. Cécile herself brings to mind the untutored twins who inhabit her novel *Echo* and who live outside their castle in Scotland, preferring the rule of nature (not always a kindly rule) to the artificial habits of society. Alfonzo's final predicament comes close to that of the unromantic Nigel Benson, poised agonisingly between family loyalty and the possibility of love, in *Hunt the Slipper*. In many of her novels Trefusis contrasts the opportunity and risk of an emotionally fulfilled life with the secure attachment to property, wealth and respectability.

In *The Hook in the Heart* she experiments with various stylistic devices that were to be carried into later novels. She tries out what became a habit of bringing together similar-sounding words with very different meanings, for example 'booty' and 'beauty' – a nice problem for translators. She also quotes the correspondence between her characters to alter the tone and focus of her narrative, giving it a more intimate and revelatory atmosphere. These letters also change the direction of the plot when they are purloined or written deliberately to deceive the recipient.

There is more plot and action in *The Hook in the Heart* than in her other novels. And there is more explicit sex. It was this, I believe, that finally decided her not to submit the book to a publisher. Inevitably it would have risked resurrecting the scandal of her lesbian love affair with Vita Sackville-West, which had continued after Violet's marriage to Denys Trefusis and lasted into the early 1920s. There is no same-sex love in this novel, but there are other incidental connections with the past: Vita Sackville-West's grandmother, Pepita, was a famously beautiful Spanish gypsy dancer of humble origins who became the mistress of Lionel Sackville-West (later the second Baron Sackville). One of their illegitimate daughters was Vita's mother who, like the two mothers in *The Hook in the Heart*, showed her daughter little love. Spain had been active in Violet's and Vita's imaginations and is illustrated by their use of words from the Spanish Romany language as a secret code. Violet had longed to go to Spain with Vita. But Vita was unable to go and 'I couldn't stand Spain without you', Violet wrote in the summer of 1919. 'It was agony to think how you would have enjoyed things.'

These facts could be used to reduce this novel to a simple *roman-à-clef*, but this would be misleading. That her love for Vita may have occupied some place in the origins of the story seems possible. But *The Hook in the Heart,* on which she worked intermittently for a number of years, is very far from being a slice of autobiographical fiction – indeed it is an example of how she widened her focus, reinterpreted the past and used her imagination to create sharply differentiated characters. She also added some fine moments of comedy to the romantic narrative (for example, the gypsy's ridiculous new clothes, bought by selling the jewellery belonging to the family of his lover's husband).

A similar theme is explored in *Tandem,* written by Trefusis in her late thirties. Like *Pirates at Play,* her last novel published in 1950 and set in Italy, the opening chapter is crowded with a bewildering number of characters. At the centre of this crowd is a Greek family living in France. The head of this family is the tiny polite Madame Demetriades, who has a strange resemblance to an umbrella. She is the mother of three young daughters whom she treats paradoxically as if she were their child. They are accompanied by a couple of governesses, one who resembles a horse, the other who looks like a crow, and also by an 'aunt' who is really a cousin and an uncle who manufactures perfumes. They inhabit a gloomy and eccentric mansion on the French Riviera called the Villa Ivanhoe, which may be seen as an ironic backward glance at the antiquated pseudo-Scottish castle where Trefusis set her earlier novel *Echo.* The reader is also introduced to the memory of one masculine character, Madame Demetriades's unfaithful husband Perikles, who mercifully is dead. He stands in for, and is an allusion to, Ernest Beckett, the second Lord Grimthorpe, who was an English banker, traveller, Member of Parliament and, in the words of the Irish novelist George Moore, 'London's greatest lover'. Beckett had several illegitimate children, one of whom is generally thought to be Violet herself (he having had a love affair with Alice Keppel before she became the mistress of the Prince of Wales, later Edward VII). Ernest Beckett absented himself from his illegitimate daughter's life – and, in retaliation as it were, Perikles is quickly removed from these pages.

When we first meet the three daughters of Madam Demetriades they are described as being like a family of tiny bright birds 'twittering and preening behind the bars of a cage'. The novel follows them as they escape from their cage and fly away. The eldest daughter is the monolithic Marguerite. With her large, tactless feet and perfect digestion (considered by the others as being slightly vulgar), she looms unsympathetically over the rest of this small, gifted family. But she gives no trouble and excites no interest (even in her mother), and soon vanishes from the story after marrying a wealthy nonentity with vague political ambitions. We leave her as she prepares to settle down to a life devoted to her cooking and her children. This is a rather wicked pen portrait-in-miniature of Violet's sister Sonia (the two sisters did not speak to each other for the first ten years of their lives together).

Tandem covers seventy years (from 1892 to 1962), during which we follow the lives of the two other sisters, Pénélope, who becomes a brilliant writer, and Irène, who is an acute observer. They marry within a fortnight of each other, Pénélope to a French and Irène to an English aristocrat. Before their marriages they appear as 'disarmingly alike', like twins, especially when they wear the same clothes – and they may be said to represent two aspects of Violet Trefusis, who uses their stories to forecast what might have happened to her had she lived in and absorbed the culture of England as opposed to France.

Some of the most amusing passages in the novel come from the pages that tell Irène's life story in three different forms: as letters to her mother, passages from her confidential diary and a third-person narrative by the author. The letters and diaries, written in a great country house in Dorset (mysteriously smelling of strawberry jam) excel at contrasting French and English manners and giving examples of the hostility that cordially persists between them – France being, according to the English, a country through which they must quickly pass 'in order to reach Italy'.

Irène's diary also introduces a new female character called Nancy into the novel. She attempts to change the event-plot of this part of the book so that it eclipses comedy with tragedy. She is described in words that were later to be repeated in Trefusis's memoir *Don't Look Round*. This enables us to identify Nancy as Pat Dansey, a false friend of Violet's who had secretly helped to alienate Vita. Her character in this novel is more devious and hostile than the amusing description of her in the memoir. 'I can't make out whether she likes me or not,' Irène writes in her diary. In time Nancy reveals herself as a dangerous enemy whose circuitous plots are principally designed to hurt people. 'I ought to have guessed long ago,' Irène concludes, echoing what Violet herself must have felt.

The last half of *Tandem* examines whether Irène's safety-first temperament and Pénélope's ambitious talent were advantageous or detrimental to their happiness. Did their marriages, their positions in society, give them emotional fulfilment? Both of them were Greek by origin – and the novel questions whether, like some wines, they travelled well or became aliens in France and England. As she steers the story into the future, Trefusis charts the effects of aging and the nearness of death. In fiction, she suggests, women become charming old ladies with adoring grandchildren. They lose their petals gracefully one by one until one day their hearts stop beating: 'that is all'. In no culture other than Greece, the land of the *Iliad* and the *Odyssey*, 'was death so ignored [and] in such low repute', she writes. But elsewhere, and in reality, death has not lost its sting and old age becomes horrific. The passages that predict this, similar to passages in *Don't Look Round*, show the darkness that is part of Trefusis's literary imagination.

In a letter to Vita Sackville-West in November 1932, Virginia Woolf wrote of Violet Trefusis coming to see her. 'It was her novel that brought her here,' she writes, adding that she will explain why exactly she came 'if you'll keep it a secret'. A footnote in *The Sickle Side of the Moon: The Letters of Virginia Woolf, 1932–1935* refers readers to *Tandem*, the implication being that Trefusis was attempting to get her novel published by Leonard and Virginia Woolf's Hogarth Press and that it had been rejected. But looking carefully at the dates, it seems more likely that she had come to discuss her next novel, *Broderie Anglaise*. This was to be a riposte to Virginia Woolf's *Orlando*, a novel which had been dedicated to Vita and contained a wonderfully fantastical Russian princess inspired by Vita's description of Violet (and possibly by some of Violet's letters to her, which she had shown Virginia).

Tandem was published by Heinemann in the early summer of 1933, six months after Violet had met Virginia. In it Trefusis had contrasted French and English taste by describing their gardens, calling the former beautifully designed and symmetrical and the latter a jungle tangled with all sorts of surprising flowers and strange beasts. Written in English and dedicated to her mother, *Tandem* is that tangled garden; and *Broderie Anglaise,* written in French (which Violet's mother did not read) is a well-designed symmetrical garden. The novel is dedicated to no one, and was not translated by Barbara Bray into English until 1986 – long after Virginia and Vita, Violet and her mother, were all dead.

Orlando is a fantasy about history and contemporary life and a satire on biography – the sort of biography that Woolf herself was to write about her friend Roger Fry. 'My own lyric vein is to be satirised,' she wrote in her diary on 14 March 1927, shortly before beginning the novel. Her lyric vein was to be supremely employed in the opening chapter of *Orlando,* where she writes of Sasha, with whom Orlando falls desperately in love – and who owes her fictional existence to Violet. Woolf's own emotional life had been fragile and precarious. Critics mention the fact that early in 1909 the homosexual Lytton Strachey proposed marriage to her. What is perhaps more significant was that she accepted his proposal – before the two of them thought better of it. Later on Strachey prepared the ground for Leonard Woolf's proposal after he returned to England from Ceylon. Theirs was to be a *mariage blanc* – a prudent and protective arrangement that did not endanger her. With Vita, on the other hand, Virginia enjoyed the most open sexual experience of her life, though she made sure it did not get out of control and cause a breakdown. The affair between Vita and Violet had been far more torrid and intense – something that Virginia never experienced but which stimulated her imagination in *Orlando.*

Sasha is made for loving – an extraordinary seductiveness issues from her whole person. She and Orlando increasingly desired each other's presence and their intimacy, which became a scandal at court, dramatically changed Orlando. He would 'take her in his arms, and know, for the first time, he murmured, the delights of love'. But below this passion moved an undercurrent of dark fore-bodings. For all Sasha's voluptuous openness, Orlando suspected something was being concealed from him, something hidden. 'What was her father? Had she brothers?' Perhaps her social position was not so high as she would have liked. Was there not 'something rank in her, something coarse-flavoured, something peasant born?' Seeing her on the knees of a large, muscular sailor, Orlando had difficulty accepting her innocent explanation and comforted himself imagining how she would grow fat, unwieldy and lethargic by the age of forty. But his jealousy mounted. As Sasha escapes over the horizon in her Russian ship, its 'black eagles flying over the mast-head', Orlando is left hurling 'at the faithless woman all the insults that have ever been the lot of her sex'.

There is no factual record of what Violet Trefusis thought of this story when she read the first chapter of *Orlando* or of what she and Woolf had said to each other when they met. Both appear to have been enthusiastically polite, Violet inviting Virginia to visit her in France and Virginia writing to Vita: 'I quite see now why you were so enamoured – then ... what seduction! What a voice – lisping, faltering, what warmth, suppleness...' The Sasha who would grow fat and unwieldy at forty is predicted by Woolf's description of Violet Trefusis in her thirty-ninth year as 'a little too full, now, rather overblown'. Behind their politeness and a natural curiosity lies some discord between Vita's two lovers.

Broderie Anglaise is in part a criticism of and variant text to *Orlando*: what Trefusis called 'a corrective'. Woolf appears in this novel as the famous author Alexa Harrowby Quince, a tall, contemplative woman of thirty-seven who, writing with her head rather than her heart and fearful that facts might hamper her imagination, creates an artificially romantic story in her novel *Conquest*. She has been helped in the writing of it by her lover Lord Shorne (based on Vita Sackville-West). He is a sombre, 29-year-old 'Prince Charming' who has supplied her with telling details about the great love of his life: the false but ravishing Anne Lindell – an imaginary vision of Violet. Being 'the only one that mattered' in Lord Shorne's story, this fictional figure casts a dark shadow over Alexa's heart.

There are several descriptions of Alexa that would not have pleased Woolf. Her faded and unfeminine figure has none of the physical seductiveness that animated *Orlando*'s Sasha. In her introduction to the first British edition of *Broderie Anglaise*, Vita Sackville-West's biographer, Victoria Glendinning, points to people's hair being used by Trefusis as a symbol of sensuality. Alexa's hair is described as thin, scanty, modest, listless and unenterprising: 'my hair's taboo' she tells Lord Shorne. Trefusis has much fun describing the limpness of her clothes that 'lent her movements the undulation of a sea-anemone. She was fluid and elusive; a piece of water-weed, a puff of smoke'. This narrow and unhappy figure, with her nostalgic hats and timid little handbag, is set amid the frills and flounces of a Bloomsbury Group decoration.

Lord Shorne's name suggests he is shorn of all hair. His countenance is an English version of the hereditary features of Alfonzo, the Spanish Duke of Cantijo in *The Hook in the Heart*. He has no sensuality and is attracted by Alexa's virginal air and the fact that her literary talent has made her 'one of the most distinguished women in England'. Alexa is attracted to him because his hereditary face has come, 'eternally bored, through five centuries' of one of his country's most illustrious families. Their love has blossomed in England where 'the driving force is snobbery'. Lord Shorne is by far the more secure and powerful of the two, Alexa being tormented by her uncertainty. 'Why don't you ever surprise me?' he asks her. The novel shows how the unexpected appearance of Anne Lindell has armed Alexa with a chance of gaining ascendancy.

Alexa believes she knows this woman with a past, having already created her 'every feature, every tone of voice' in her novel. But Anne arrives full of surprises. She is not the ravishing beauty of whom Lord Shorne had spoken, despite her mass of thick springy hair and soft crepuscular voice. What she brings to the story is a revelatory truth about Lord Shorne's mother, a vividly described matriarch owing much to Lady Sackville, Vita Sackville-West's mother, and playing a similar role to Alfonzo's witch-like grandmother, the dowager duchess, in *The Hook in the Heart*.

Anne Lindell (who has written two books) admires Alexa's novels, but criticises *Conquest*. Why did Alexa make the woman in it (i.e. Sasha) 'someone false and treacherous', she asks, 'when really she's only an impulsive little animal?' Alexa is vexed at having believed everything Lord Shorne told her. The conquest now belongs to Anne. The two women breathe the scent of a flower that is sharper than love. They are sisters in revenge.

Against Woolf's timeless fantasy of history and gender, Trefusis offers an ingenious discourse that questions the freedoms of modernist fiction and offers an alternative view of the literary landscape.

A High Wind in Jamaica

I first read Richard Hughes's *A High Wind in Jamaica* in my early teens – not much older than the eldest child in the novel. I thought it was a wonderful book, full of excitement and adventure. I was enthralled by the violent destruction of the thunderstorm and the mysterious behaviour of the earthquake. I also loved the pantomime pirates and the surreal sea voyages to and from exotic islands. And then what a tremendous supernumerary cast of animals and insects there were! – turtles and wild cats, snakes, pigs, monkeys, winged cockroaches and suckerfish as well as a lion, a tiger and a miniature crocodile. I had never read a book with such an amazing crew of characters.

I was some fifty years older when I read the book again: a different person reading a different novel; sinister, darker, more poignant and complex. *A High Wind in Jamaica* is one of those rare novels that works on more than one level and can appeal to all ages. It changes as we change, and its theme is change itself.

Changes of all kinds fill the novel. In the first chapter we are introduced to the social and cultural changes that took place in Jamaica during the nineteenth century. Later we witness the accidental, split-second change from life to death on board the *Clorinda,* and also, when the ship lands, the apparently magical change of women into men. Then there is a most dramatic change that overtakes everyone at the parochial bazaar on St Lucia after a few gallons of an enticing alcoholic drink called Hangman's Blood has been passed all round. To the children's eyes, the whole nature of the adults 'seemed to be breaking up, like ice melting ... The tone of their voices changed, and they began to talk much slower, to move more slowly and elaborately. The expression of their faces became more candid, and yet more mask-like: hiding less, there was also less to hide.'

These changes, and many others, are used to illustrate the unbridgeable divide between children and adults. They inhabit parallel worlds that are indeed hidden from one another, worlds with different timescales, odd priorities and contradictory values. The awful storm that destroys their parents' house creates a paradise for the children – a perfect playground. The only tragedy is the death of a tabby cat. For these children the one reality is their eternal present – the past becomes easily forgotten and the future is always fantastical. But adults require sophisticated calculations to be made from precedents and foresight in order to discover their precarious reality. 'It is a fact that it takes experience before one can realise what is a catastrophe and what is not,' Richard Hughes ironically explains. With the aid of this experience the children's father charts a journey for them to escape the dangers of the natural world and reach the mythical safety of an adult world.

A forecast of what will happen is given in the opening chapter. When Emily was aged eight, her mother

had thought she was too big to bathe naked any more. The only bathing-dress she could rig was an old cotton nightgown. Emily jumped in as usual: first the balloons of air tipped her upside down, and then the wet cotton wrapped itself round her head and arms and nearly drowned her. After that, decency was let go hang: it was hardly worth being drowned for – at least it did not at first sight appear to be.

But then, at the age of ten, sitting up to her chin in a bathing-hole, Emily suddenly feels 'hundreds of infant fish tickling with their inquisitive mouths every inch of her body, a sort of expressionless light kissing'. Here, in miniature, is the theme of the novel and the first touch of adulthood, which Emily finds 'abominable'.

A High Wind in Jamaica was Richard Hughes's first novel. It was written over a peculiarly anxious and difficult period of his life when he was in his mid- to late twenties. His engagement to a young poet, Nancy Stallibrass, had been broken off a few days before the date of the wedding, and he suffered a nervous collapse. In his depression he was able to write for not more than 'ten minutes at a time' and often found that he could not 'write at all for days together'.

He began, however, borrowing his friends' children, inviting them to stay with him and finding, as he later wrote, small children 'to be almost the only human characters I could tolerate'. Getting to know these children apart from their parents was a great stimulus for his novel. His erotic interest in prepubescent girls is mirrored by a scene in chapter six where Jonsen, the pirate captain, puts one hand under the thirteen-year-old Emily's chin and begins to stroke her hair with the other. 'A sort of vertigo seized her,' Richard Hughes writes: 'she caught his thumb and bit it as hard as she could: then, terrified at her own madness, dashed across the hold to where the other children were gathered in a wondering knot.'

But this dash back to absolute childhood is no longer quite possible and the other children ostracise her for behaving so badly. Captain Jonsen, ashamed of his momentary weakness and the sinister possibilities it reveals, mistakes Emily's later behaviour for hostility. But she misunderstands his avoidance of her and blames herself for the instinctive violence to what was apparently a friendly gesture. Not ready yet for this journey into the adult world, she lies incoherently in a limbo between childhood and adulthood. Their relationship is subtly changed and Emily, in a panic of remorse, begins to flirt outrageously with the captain and his mate. At the conclusion, Richard Hughes prepares for the paedophiliac tendencies he has seen lurking in himself and transferred to Captain Jonsen – a fictional warning for what might have developed into fact, and a form of atonement.

The novel was first published in the United States in March 1929 with a title that the author had chosen, *The Innocent Voyage*. It appeared later that same year in Britain as *A High Wind in Jamaica*. In both countries reviewers praised the charm and originality of the book. Ford Madox Ford wrote that the author's literary gift lay in the 'sheer magic of implication'. Nowhere was this gift more imaginatively exercised than over the fate of the thirteen-year-old Creole girl, Margaret Fernandez. 'It ought to be perfectly clear to you what has happened,' her aunt says. But Margaret herself says nothing and her behaviour is thought to be very puzzling by the other children. Unlike Emily, she has not dashed back to them, but spends her time in secret with the sailors. As Ford Madox Ford warned his readers, the implications that Richard Hughes handled with such mastery are not comfortable.

After a slow beginning, the novel sold very well. In 1965 Alexander Mackendrick made an enjoyable if rather sentimental film of it (best remembered now perhaps for the appearance of Martin Amis as one of the children). By the time Martin Amis grew up and came to read the novel, describing it as 'a thrillingly good book', *A High Wind in Jamaica* had acquired the status of a classic.

In his biography of Richard Hughes, Richard Percival Graves placed the novel between R. M. Ballantyne's optimistic adventure story *The Coral Island* published in 1856, which shows a group of children cast away on a deserted atoll 'to be naturally good, decent and self-reliant', and William Golding's *Lord of the Flies*, published almost a hundred years later, in which the civilised values of adult society are soon jettisoned by the schoolboys who turn to savagery on their island. *A High Wind in Jamaica* takes no sides as it patrols the eccentric, sometimes amoral borders between a child's and an adult's natural territory.

Richard Hughes's career was irregular and did not help to give him easy recognition as a writer. Starting out as a poet, he had turned to writing plays, became a novelist, went on to write short stories for both children and adults, and did not publish his second novel until 1938. *In Hazard,* which took the same subject as Conrad's *Typhoon,* contains some strong pages of narrative description, as well as intimate particulars of engine rooms and details of meteorology. 'It is full of remarkable things,' Virginia Woolf wrote. 'It seems to me possible that on the one hand there's the storm: on the other the people. And between them there's a gap.' This described very well what I myself felt when I read the book in the late 1960s. I admired much of it, but could not feel engaged as I had with his first novel.

He did not publish his next novel for twenty-two years. *A Fox in the Attic* was planned as the opening volume of a tetralogy bearing the portentous title *The Human Predicament*. I remember reading it at the same time as *In Hazard* before going to stay with the author in 1970. It was an impressive and unusual historical novel, based on lengthy research, containing a medley of fictional and actual characters, and chronicling the rise of Hitler's Nazism. The book had a similar divergence of tone – what Kenneth Allsop called 'the sinister and the frolicsome' – with that which he had employed so brilliantly in *A High Wind in Jamaica*.

I went to stay with Richard and his wife Frances (a painter mainly, or so I gathered, of bonfires and waterfalls) for a few rainswept days at Môr Edrin, a remote house, almost islanded it appeared, which they had bought after the war from the architect Clough Williams-Ellis. It lay like a ship at anchor, on the opposite side of the estuary from Portmeirion. I was writing my biography of Augustus John, who had used Richard and Frances's home nearby at Laugharne Castle House during the 1920s and 1930s as a staging post on journeys to his elderly father in Tenby (journeys he dreaded and sometimes failed to complete). I remember Richard telling me that John had complained, with some indignation, that his father was on his deathbed, but refused to get into it.

The regime at Môr Edrin struck me as being dedicated and regular. Richard, then aged seventy, a tall, white-bearded, enigmatic figure dressed, as I recall, in an oatmeal jacket and trousers, would go into his study in the morning, where he was writing and rewriting the second volume of *The Human Predicament*, to be called *The Wooden Shepherdess*. Nothing was allowed to disturb him. I formed the opinion that, were the house to suddenly go up in flames, his oatmeal figure would remain at the desk, writing and rewriting, gloriously illuminated by the fire all round him – while Frances eagerly took the opportunity to paint a really splendid picture.

But later in my visit I saw another side of Richard. He recounted with, I now see, all his playwriting skills, a spectacular castle farce that had taken place at Laugharne in the mid-1930s. The dramatic personae included, besides Augustus John and Hughes himself (as a stage narrator who supplies the story), the beautiful fiery Caitlin Macnamara and the not-wholly sober Dylan Thomas. Laugharne, he explained to me, while laying out the *mise en scène,* was somewhat roofless, which offered the actors novel opportunities, but had a good cellar to keep them going, a useful watchtower for the narrator, and plenty of surrounding shrubbery – some of it with the damaged advantage of being haunted. It also had three good traditional entrance doors. I took some notes of what he said.

No sooner had Dylan gone out by one of these doors than John would appear through another. Though the plot was confused, a tremendous atmosphere of melodrama built up. Caitlin was on stage for most of the performance, but when the exigencies of the theatre demanded it, she would make a quick exit, while the two men made their entrances. The timing throughout was remarkable, and there were many rhetorical monologues in the high-flown style. To the spectators, wiping their eyes, the outcome was uncertain. But, a year later, Caitlin married Dylan at the Penzance register office; and when their first child was born, Hughes and John were godfathers.

There was also an epilogue in the form of a christening service at which John, by then very deaf and somewhat misunderstanding his role, broke out at intervals with the refrain, 'I desire it!'

In the telling of this story (which I begged him to repeat – he was especially good when taking on the part of Caitlin), it appeared as if some batteries within him suddenly became switched on and he came alive with the illuminating humour and spellbinding charm I recognised from *A High Wind in Jamaica* – especially since his story possessed shadowy sexual happenings backstage that gave the piece a sombre dramatic quality.

Over the next five or six years I used to see him occasionally at parties in London. He always came up to me, a sympathetic but shy presence with whom it was difficult sometimes to strike up an easy conversation. It was as if this silence guarded his luminous talent which, like a genie in a bottle, could be let out only when a magic code released it, to play what awful games it might – as it had in his masterpiece *A High Wind in Jamaica*.

Dark Comedy and Entertaining Tragedy

Do you know the novels of Dan Rhodes? I ask because his books would appeal, I believe, to many readers. But he avoids journalism, does not belong to any literary groups or contemporary schools of writing and is very much an individual novelist. He neither pursues fame, nor does he patronise his readers. What he believes is what you get: sensitivity, humour, sadness and devastating shock. Sometimes I have been so saddened, so shocked, that I have stopped reading and put the book aside. But before long I was compelled to pick it up again and read on. And what I have read has found a place in my imagination.

I have never met Dan Rhodes, but have followed the outlines of his career. He was born in 1972, spent his early years in Kent and Devon and went to the Polytechnic of Wales (now the University of Glamorgan), where he took a creative-writing course led by Helen Dunmore. Later he went on the master's course there. His personal tutor was Sheenagh Pugh (who is acknowledged in his first novel). What she and others did was to edit what he wrote and, although he took 'an unpleasantly gladiatorial approach to the classes', he acknowledges that he learnt how to write succinctly and clearly – though not how to get published.

The next chapter in his career was teaching publishers how and why they should publish him. His first book contained 101 stories each of exactly 101 words. It had the title *Anthropology: And a Hundred Other Stories* and was turned down by several publishers before being brought out in 2000. This was followed by a second collection of comic and unsettling stories of sex and romance, *Don't Tell Me the Truth About Love,* which he had written at university. There were, he later explained, four main reasons for writing his early books: to impress pretty girls; to make fun of his own romantic vicissitudes; to earn some money; and to entertain people.

His first novel, *Timoleon Vieta Come Home,* is a more ambitious and demanding work. It was published in 2003, and earned him a place among the Twenty Best Young British Novelists chosen by *Granta.* But being conscripted into this ramshackle Falstaffian army and put on public parade was not his style. He felt uncomfortable and out of step. The title of his novel was taken from the T to V volume of an encyclopaedia (from Timoleon, a fourth-century Greek soldier who murdered his brother and liberated Sicily, to Franciscus Vieta, a sixth-century mathematician who anticipated modern algebra).

Five years before the story begins, an eponymous black mongrel with large ears and eyes 'as pretty as a little girl's' had arrived at a farmhouse in Umbria. The owner, a disgraced homosexual composer called Cockroft, who lives there in retirement, comes to love this mongrel, talking to it as if a human being. But a few pages into the novel another stranger arrives, a Bosnian who has never been to Bosnia. He is a disagreeable and dangerous man, but also tall and handsome, and he pays his rent every Wednesday evening with a delirious act of fellatio. Unfortunately the two visitors, man and dog, hate each other so violently that Cockroft is obliged to evict one of them. The Bosnian has a solution to the problem. He had been taught to kill dogs at school. 'They feel nothing,' he explains. 'I think maybe they enjoy it.' Cockroft persuades himself that he has been preventing a wild animal from enjoying wild adventures and decides to leave Timoleon Vieta at the Colosseum in Rome, an aesthetically pleasing place with other dogs to talk to and cats to chase and plenty of food from tourists. He will have the time of his life.

The following two thirds of the book is a modern version of Eric Knight's 1940 bestseller *Lassie Come Home.* Our irresistible mongrel soon acquires many other names – Abbondio, Teg and Leonardo da Vinci among others – given by people in whose lives he briefly appears over the forty-nine days of his travels home. Approaching his destination he has become bone-thin and moves like a ghost dog, his beautiful eyes increasingly worried. Everything ends dramatically where it began: outside the farmhouse in Umbria.

Love is also the theme of Dan Rhodes's second novel, *Gold* (2007). Here he explores its mysteries and anxieties and introduces us to those who have learnt how to exist without it. The story is centred in the Anchor, a public house on the coast of Pembrokeshire, where we get to know its regular drinkers. They are like shadows who have found shelter there.

It is not surprising that Dan Rhodes admires Chekhov. He has his own way of interweaving tragedy and comedy. They are two sides of the same coin – what one feels and what one thinks – and can come down on either side when he spins his stories.

The main character in *Gold* is Miyuki Woodward, an apparently Japanese girl who is actually Welsh. She has been coming to the Anchor for some eight or nine years now, not seeking adventure, but avoiding worry. She is a lesbian and lives happily with Grindl in a small town in one of the Welsh valleys. They are interior decorators. Twice each year one or the other goes away on holiday. Grindl goes to crowded cities abroad for her two weeks – and we never know what she is feeling. Miyuki comes to this small village on the Pembrokeshire coast – and we do know her feelings.

Despite herself, she has grown closer to these drinkers and their Monday quizzes. Their opponents, The Children from Previous Relationships, are musicians who have never played in public nor practised in private. Nor have they ever won a quiz – except on the famous evening when the other team failed to arrive. Their leader is Septic Barry, who gets his name from maintaining septic tanks. He is a master in the art of romance. He warns his team that during the following ten months they must practise their music and finally play it in public for his wedding. Knowing that all good things have to end, they reluctantly agree.

But why shouldn't good things last and bad things end? This is the question that Miyuki asks herself and it leads to a daring experiment. On clear evenings one of the rocks in the cove below lights up for a few minutes as if it had turned to gold. This golden moment, she believes, gives passers-by a glimpse of happiness before it vanishes. But does it have to vanish? Could she not do something to improve on nature? Her plan is to become an external decorator and spray a skin of golden paint over the magic rock. But she is overcome by an avalanche of sneezes reminiscent of the famous nursery rhyme:

> Ring-a-ring of roses,
> A pocket full of posies,
> A-tishoo! A-tishoo!
> We all fall down.

For a decade Dan Rhodes has been writing his version of *The Divine Comedy*. The Anchor was his purgatory. And in his next novel *Little Hands Clapping* (2010), he invites us to visit hell. This is the darkest and most terrifying of his novels, set in an undistinguished German museum which, despite the owner's devastating good intentions, encourages visitors to hide themselves away at closing time and then commit suicide. Each room of the museum is numbered and has a cautionary theme: 'Famous Failures', 'Unfortunate Survivors' – and there is a parade of brilliant writers on view, from Sylvia Plath to Virginia Woolf.

But what is that crunchy sound you may hear early in the first chapter? It is the old grey caretaker in his narrow bed slowly devouring a live house spider that has darted into his mouth as they often do at night. He will have to get up early next morning, having heard some familiar sounds downstairs. It will be his duty to superintend matters: carefully take down the body hanging from the rope he has supplied, then ring the doctor, summon the police and also help the doctor drive the corpse away to his macabre group of freezers at home. But please, gentle reader, do not be upset. It may be an act of mercy: after all, there is very little struggle and a final end to pain. And there are no criminals involved – simply some small financial gain for the curator now that the visitors no longer need the money they had when they entered the museum.

So how do we define hell? It is where people without emotion, humanity or imagination live.

Dan Rhodes's fifth novel, *This is Life* (2012), has a very different atmosphere. It is essentially a happy book, a farewell to tragedy. One of the characters has bought a translation of *Timoleon Vieta Come Home* 'to depress a friend of mine who's been a bit too happy lately', he explains. Although love is triumphant, there is no sentimentality in the writing – it is a masterpiece of storytelling. Within the novel, *This is Life* is a hugely successful theatre presentation where for many weeks and months a man and a woman can do what we all do: make love, get out of bed, go to the toilet, have breakfast and so on, day after day. Audiences are mesmerised when they see it – and what it means to be alive. For here, mirroring their own lives though without any clouds of darkness, they may catch a vision of heaven.

Dan Rhodes has never believed that publishers are a writer's best friend. That has not been his experience. But for his most recent novel, *When the Professor got Stuck in the Snow*, he found a perfect publisher: he brought it out himself. Now a new imprint, Aardvark Bureau, has taken over its publication. I have been warned not to give away the plot. All I may say is that it is a variation of Voltaire's *Candide* – and I hope someone will soon make a musical of it.

Alexander Masters

The trouble with most twentieth-century biographers was that they focused on well-known people 'pounding through facts from grandma to the grave', wrote Alexander Masters. They were, he added, 'missing the point'. What, then, was the point? There were in fact two points: first that 'any subject that is good for fiction is good for biography', and the second was that modern biography should not follow other people's lives without revealing their own. In *Stuart: A Life Backwards,* published in 2005, Masters had set out to explore the life of a wholly unknown man whom he had met begging on a street in Cambridge. He was sitting on a square of cardboard, a wretched figure, his body in fragments. 'I had to get down on my knees to hear him speak.'

According to his mother, Stuart Shorter had been 'a real happy-go-lucky little boy' until the age of twelve, after which he became for the next twenty years a 'thief, hostage-taker, psycho and socio-pathic street raconteur'. In short he was, from Masters's point of view, 'a man with an important life'. He had been found living in and out of skips, was then given methadone to release him from heroin and began a new chapter of his life in a 'cramped, dank little apartment'. It was a strange entry into ordinary life – inter-rupted by some radical attacks on the furniture. Masters would talk to him and eventually showed him the dog-eared manuscript of his biography. 'It's bollocks boring,' Stuart told him. '… Do it the other way round. … Write it backwards.'

To Masters's astonishment this turned out to be an inspiration. It solved 'the major problem of writing a biography of a man who is not famous'. So the book was created by the subject and the writer together – and with one other person thanked in the book's acknowledgements. Without Dido Davies 'I could not have got past the first pages', he wrote.

Dido Davies was also a writer, and in 1990 had published one of those biographies Masters had described and derided about semi-well-known public people. Her subject was the novelist William Gerhardie and although Dido did not bring herself into the narrative, she had known him. In fact, I first met her (with her mother) at Gerhardie's home in London several years earlier and was able to give her some help with her book about this talented and eccentric figure. It was not until now that I noticed at the end of her acknowledgements a tribute to Alexander Masters for his 'patient attention, his careful editing, but above all his innumerable helpful and sensitive suggestions which improved the whole tone of the book'.

Stuart: A Life Backwards has already found its place in the history of biography. 'The shock opening immediately announces a new kind of personal confrontation between biographer and subject,' wrote Richard Holmes in his reflections on biography, *This Long Pursuit* (2016). 'It will be fraught, informal, no holds barred, but with extraordinary possibilities of good humour and even, eventually, mutual understanding.' He likened this 'strange duet' to Samuel Johnson's *Life of Mr Richard Savage,* his friend the poet and convicted murderer.

Among the prizes was the *Guardian* First Book Award and I was invited to the *Guardian* party. Alexander arrived with a girl called Flora, who stood by him while he made his speech. Dido Davies was also there. She came up to me indicating that she was equipped with a pearl-handled revolver, which she would aim at Masters if he failed to acknowledge her help. She had been drinking quite a lot and I edged away in case she shot the wrong person. But all was well.

Masters's next subject was Simon Phillips Norton, an Old Etonian who lurked in the basement of the biographer's old house. 'Simon has been pacing down there for twenty-seven years, three months, five days, thirteen hours and eight minutes,' he calculated on page 6 of his new book *The Genius in my Basement.* One day Simon wandered upstairs and met Stuart going through his life backwards. Often dressed in rags, Simon's genius lay in maths, plucking patterns out of chaos, spotting invisible coincidences. He became a world expert on a mathematical problem so complex and shocking that it became known as 'the Monster'. But one day he made a small mistake – and this was the beginning of the end.

Simon was left with two residual interests: politics and the time-tables of public transport. He gave much money to a campaign for transport activism and enjoyed taking buses and trains where he could meet people he need never see again. He also gave £10,000 to a member of Plane Stupid, an environmental protest group, who had attempted to glue his hand to Gordon Brown's jacket at a party in Downing Street. In short, he was an even more challenging subject for a biographer than Stuart Shorter. How then could he be chased into a book? It seemed as unlikely as Simon solving the Monster's intractable problem. Both had impossible tasks – but two minuses make a plus. 'By the end of this book,' Masters had predicted, 'it's likely I shall be writing about someone entirely different from the man with whom I began.' And so it was.

Alexander Masters is an artist as well as a writer. His book on Stuart was full of charming drawings of him, where he was and what he was doing. Simon's career was more challenging and included some baffling mathematical drawings too. The reviews were enthusiastic. 'A comical tender portrait ... captivating ... wholly original ... an antidote to the celebrity memoirs ... has the magic power of Sherlock Holmes ...' But it did not attract such large sales as his previous book, which had been turned into a successful BBC film. Perhaps some would-be readers felt nervous of mathematics – besides, this second book could not have the novelty of his first.

It was published in 2011 – while his third book had been waiting for him some ten years after its contents had been fished out of a skip near where Simon lived. Among the bricks and slates, the wet tree stumps and a broken shower tray that had been tossed into this metal skip were some diaries – 148 of them in all sorts and sizes – from which a detective story would gradually emerge. There was to be no one's name in the title of this book: it was simply *A Life Discarded*.

These diaries had been written with great urgency and a mechanical regularity between the 1950s and 1990s. Alexander calculates that the owner must have written 2,500 words a day, every day, including those days in which the diaries were lost. The words are scribbled all over the page, often in tiny writing 'as pale as a whisper'. This made his job no easier as he confronted over a million words of anonymous writing. As a literary detective, he presents himself as a wonderfully comic figure. With great ingenuity he studies several passages in order to calculate the height of his biographical subject. It turns out to be far taller than any human being has ever reached. He calls the writer It before deciding that it must be a man or woman, in which case it is almost certainly a man. For several chapters he is definitely a man. But after some more detective work in libraries he sees the correct name could have been Mary – only to discover that the Mary he has in his sights was not after all the diary owner. So her new name becomes Not Mary. This turns out to be good news, because one day when in a violent temper Not Mary attempts to kill someone (possibly himself) with a knife, our biographer discovers he is suffering from the curse of 'my sex' which explains the blood in the room and confirms that 'he's a woman'. Alexander manages to get a picture of her at school, but she is among seventy other girls, none of them named.

No wonder our biographer decides to employ a detective and a couple of graphologists. The detective discovers that a very elderly friend of Not Mary's was a Dame. This worries Alexander. He does not want his subject to become an aristocrat. There were other surprises too. He is astonished when one of the graphologists, after studying the diary writing carefully, declared that Not Mary's birthday must have been on 22 May 1939. How, Alexander asked her, could she tell this? She answers that it was written by Not Mary in a paragraph he had not yet reached. So he reads her birthday entries in her diaries from 1952 to 2001 – a downward journey beginning with a list of presents, good spirits and a lovely dream, which then descends into uncelebrated days and one at the age of forty-five, a day she completely forgets. 'I wonder if it would have been better,' she wrote, 'if I had died.' She was, Masters believes, 'a child trapped in an adult's body'.

One of Masters's strengths as a writer is his ability to marry tragedy with comedy. Like him, Not Mary was an artist as well as a writer and the pages of this book are lit up by both their drawings. About three quarters into the book, he discovers the name of his subject and a little later the fact that she is in her seventies and happily alive. This could of course lead to copyright complications. In fact she did not object to what he wrote and he was to give her 25 per cent of his royalties on the book. A perfect agreement. Even at the age of eighteen she was telling her diary that she wanted to be 'a writer of merit, perhaps even fame'. And now her biographer has brought her wish alive. She has succeeded.

But there is a tragedy in the book. It was Dido Davies who had slid into the skip and brought out the diaries. She and Alexander were long-time friends. Many years earlier, as a newly elected English fellow, Dido had crawled through the window of Alexander's college and said hello. Her career was unusual. Under the name Rachel Swift she published two sexual manuals and, following her interest in zoology, travelled widely in Asia, occasionally giving lectures on rats and serpents. While Alexander was working on his book about Not Mary, she had been writing a biography of Thomas More. They helped each other and she became his 'writing collaborator', giving his books their direction. But in 2007 she was found to be suffering with cancer, which grew worse and was the cause of her death in 2013. Three years later *A Life Discarded* was published and dedicated to Dido Davies.

Pas de Deux

Isadora and Gordon Craig

The reworking of Kenneth MacMillan's celebrated ballet *Isadora* brings dramatically into public view the reputations of two phenomenal characters: the American dancer Isadora Duncan and her lover, the stage designer Edward Gordon Craig.

The idea of a ballet based on the life and career of Isadora Duncan first came to Kenneth MacMillan in the late 1960s (shortly after Craig's death and forty years since Isadora had died, tragically and ridiculously, in a blue Bugatti in Nice). But it was not until ten years later, when he saw Frederick Ashton's choreographic miniatures *Five Brahms Waltzes in the Manner of Isadora Duncan*, danced by Lynn Seymour, that the idea became a reality

A critical moment in the evolution of his ballet, making it a more theatrical and cinematic creation, took place when Ashton revealed that Isadora had spoken as well as danced during her performances. MacMillan then decided to present two Isadoras on stage: the dancer (Merle Park) and an actor (Mary Miller), who provided an explanatory narrative of the dancer's life. He discussed this idea with the novelist Gillian Freeman, who had provided a scenario for his previous ballet, *Meyerling,* and who picked out quotations for him from Isadora's romanticised autobiography, *My Life.* In addition to this she drafted several versions of a scenario based on biographies and, most significantly, on Francis Steegmuller's *Your Isadora,* a selection of Isadora's correspondence with Gordon Craig, which presents a more disturbing account of what had been the most intense love affair in her life.

MacMillan set himself some complex problems in this ambitious work. How was he to present a ballet-biography of a life so chaotically crowded with melodramatic events? And how could he show us Isadora's freestyle dancing during the early twentieth century without making her appear ridiculous to modern audiences?

He decided to focus mainly on Isadora's love affairs with three men. Her nine-minute *pas de deux* with Gordon Craig is a wonderfully sustained and ingenious piece of erotic interplay; her dance with the millionaire Paris Singer is a more formal and (when it develops into a *pas de trois*) competitive composition; and her meeting with the volatile Russian poet Sergei Esenin, whom she married, became the most violent and athletic of these duets (though, sadly to my mind, this was cut from the new version). But, representing many of her other loves, there is still the 'Give me a Child' dance with a beautiful stranger on a beach.

Perhaps the most extraordinary of these *pas de deux* is her dance of grief with Paris Singer after their son and Isadora's daughter by Gordon Craig were drowned in the Seine. The two dancers continually fall and pick each other up as they fumble and circle around the stage. It is not a beautiful sight: indeed it is deliberately awkward, and it is this ungainliness that conveys their grief in a most poignant fashion. There is no part for Craig here – he never went to the funeral of his daughter and hardly saw Isadora again.

Watching the Grenada Television programme of the ballet made in the early 1980s, it seemed to me that Isadora's solos were rather less successful. MacMillan did not make the mistake of trying to copy Isadora's actual performances in her loose, flowing costumes. He took what was for him the unusual decision of commissioning a score, choosing as his composer Richard Rodney Bennett, who came up with a clever series of imitations of Brahms, Liszt and Chopin interspersed with Scott Joplin – a witty pastiche that helped MacMillan give an impression of Isadora's dancing. But this music was not what Isadora actually used on stage and, not being quite authentic, may sometimes appear to mimic her, losing perhaps the light charm of her early pieces and the sombre mood of her late performances ('I never saw *true* tragedy before,' wrote Ellen Terry after seeing her 'Revolutionary Dance' in the summer of 1921).

Isadora's anti-formal dancing was a challenge to the rigid, straitjacket discipline of nineteenth-century classical ballet – just as Craig's innovations were an attack on the sentimental melo-dramas of London's West End theatres. Both were, in Gillian Freeman's words, 'outside contemporary society' and are still seen today as either prodigies or charlatans.

Edward Thorpe's biography of Kenneth MacMillan describes his *Isadora* as a stimulating and audacious multimedia work that divided critical opinion. 'It needs absolutely drastic cutting,' wrote the *Guardian* critic Mary Clarke. In fact MacMillan was to shorten it by some twenty minutes before the premiere in America. The present reworking, under the supervision of his widow Deborah MacMillan, should further tighten the performance, giving it added intensity by replacing the narrator–actor with a simultaneous voice-over narrative.

It is difficult to form a first-hand opinion of Isadora Duncan, since it must mainly be based on hearsay and reviews. But with Gordon Craig we have what he wrote in his magazines and books. 'No man in the English language is so hated and reviled, no man so passionately defended and revered,' wrote the Irish playwright Lennox Robinson. 'A man who can arouse such feelings of hatred and love can indubitably be no nonentity.'

What people have come to hate about Craig was his treat-ment of Isadora and the other women in his life. In any court of sexual morals he would surely have been found guilty of inflicting wanton cruelty – and of irresponsibly abandoning his children. Over thirty years, scattered through five countries, he had thirteen children by eight women. Yet some of these women, including Isadora Duncan, might object to being cast in the role of victim by a later generation.

Craig had been born in 1872 and was the illegitimate son of Ellen Terry. He could not remember his father, Edward William

Godwin, the architect friend of Whistler, whom Max Beerbohm called 'the greatest aesthete of them all'. His parents seemed to prefer his elder sister Edy – in any event, when they separated from each other both of them wanted to keep her but not him.

To be closer to his mother, he had gone on stage when young, but been overwhelmed by the powerful dramatic presence of his godfather Henry Irving, who was Ellen Terry's theatre partner and also her lover. Craig admired Irving, but knew he could never outperform him. To establish a completely different theatre, a visionary non-realistic place of the future through which he could establish a new identity, he left England in his early thirties and, much to his mother's distress, lived the rest of his life in exile.

'It is impossible to read his books, impossible to look at his designs, without being filled with a new sense of the possibilities of the theatre,' wrote James Laver, the keeper of engravings, designs and paintings at the Victoria and Albert Museum. Yet Craig's ideas seldom appeared to reach beyond possibilities and invade the living theatre.

Over sixty years in Europe he produced and designed only three plays: a brilliantly original version of *Rosmersholm* for Eleonora Duse in Florence in 1906; the famous production of *Hamlet* for Stanislavski in Moscow in 1912; and a controversial presentation of Ibsen's *The Pretenders* with Johannes Paulsen in Copenhagen in 1926.

At his workshop at Florence he experimented with screens that could be imperceptibly moved to reveal a landscape, an adjoining room, a castle courtyard. He grew ingenious at conjuring forth strange haunting shadows and producing a magic spectacle of masks, mime and abstract movement – and he advocated the power of silence.

After Craig's death in his mid-nineties, Harold Hobson, drama critic of the *Sunday Times*, wrote that there was something 'cloud-capped, mythological, Olympian about his concept of production. His mind moved into the golden world of giants, not the Welfare State. He would have filled the stage with mighty cliffs and precipices, with dreadful gulfs and lowering clouds, not with back-to-back houses and washing machines.' Though Craig scholars might take issue with this Wagnerian description and claim that he could easily have designed an imaginatively bleak and claustrophobic set for *Look Back in Anger*, it is true that Craig seemed to belong to the future or the past but seldom to the present. He deplored the popularity of Bernard Shaw's static and far-from-silent political plays, which depended for their dramatic effect on compelling argument, and attacked them in his magazine *The Mask*. Shaw retaliated by describing Craig's reputation as an illusion. 'You cared nothing about the drama, and could not feel art in dramatic terms,' he wrote to him in 1929. 'You were trying to make a picture of the proscenium, to replace actors by figures, and drive the dramatic poet out of the theatre. And as I was doing precisely the reverse ... you felt I was the arch-enemy.'

Craig was always on the lookout for enemies and nursed a morbid fear of failure. He did not trust anyone, suspecting they would steal his ideas. He even accused Isadora of plagiarising him – though what he really feared, I believe, was the pain that might follow such an overwhelming emotional experience if he did not end their affair on his terms. He risked far less than she did. Her later promiscuity is poignant, his threatening.

What Craig sought was the absolute authority he had admired in Henry Irving's Lyceum Theatre. But no theatre manager – neither Beerbohm Tree nor Max Reinhardt, who both invited him to work with them – could cede total control of their playhouses to him. He had no wish to learn from their pragmatic compromises. The *Hamlet* which Craig's German patron, Count Harry Kessler, published at the Cranach Press at the end of 1929 was less a record of the Moscow production than Craig's ideal vision of the play.

Students relished the sheer excess and anarchy of his writings, grasping at the revolutionary baton he appeared to be holding out to them. And academics were to enjoy the challenge of picking their way across the minefield of his scholarly work with all the misleading signposts he placed there to protect the integrity of his ideas against enemy invaders. He did not have the popular appeal of Isadora Duncan in her prime nor the long romantic memories she left.

What influence did they both have on contemporary dance and drama? All forms of dance have become more free, ingenious and erotic. Contemporary ballet too has escaped the straitjacket of the nineteenth century and been transformed. Yet this would inevitably have happened without Isadora. Perhaps MacMillan's *Isadora*, which is conceived in homage to her, is her greatest post-humous triumph. Barry Kay's scenic effects for the ballet, using an enormous curtain runner and stripping the stage right back to drab brick walls with a few props, were obviously inspired by Craig's theories and in retrospect may be said to have brought him and Isadora closer together.

Craig has a legendary reputation as a theorist. But film and the theatre are still governed by imitation realism rather than the symbolism he advocated– the only film I have recently seen that strongly bears his mark is Ariane Mnouchkine's *Molière.*

There is no mention I have read of Craig's influence in the reviews of this film nor in the critics' descriptions of Barry Kay's sets for *Isadora* – but that is not surprising. As Peter Brook has written: 'the ideas that Craig stated, shouted, loaded into blunderbusses and shot into the air, ideas that went to Russia, then to Germany, and eventually reached England and America … are now everyday axioms in the designer's language'. But, he added, these revolutionary concepts no longer have Craig's name attached to them.

John Stewart Collis

In the autumn of 2008 *Slightly Foxed* published an essay by Richard Ingrams, who had chosen John Stewart Collis's book called *The Worm Forgives the Plough* – a title taken from William Blake's 'Proverbs of Hell'. The book had been written (originally in two volumes with different titles) during the Second World War when Collis, then in his forties, had become one of the agricultural labourers who took the place of farm workers enlisted by the army. This was an inspiring period of his career during which he produced his literary classic – a judgement that was endorsed when in 2009 Vintage added the book to its list of classics with a compelling introduction by Robert Macfarlane.

'To work as a labourer on the land had been a great desire of mine,' Collis wrote. This was his adult education. He learnt harrowing and ditching, ploughing and haymaking and harvesting – and finally he cleared the wild entanglement of an ash wood later to be named Collis Piece. Occasionally he would revisit this wood. 'Nobody is ever likely to confer upon me Honours or Titles of city freedoms, nor will any Monument be raised to perpetuate and repeat my name,' he wrote. 'But this plot of earth will do it, these trees will do it: in the summer they will glitter and shine for me, and in the winter, mourn.'

The danger of being known as the author of a single masterpiece is that your other books may unjustly be neglected. Certainly Collis's biographies and autobiographies, his ecology and fiction are too original to be forgotten.

He was born in Killiney to the south of Dublin where his father worked as a solicitor. Collis was the younger twin, their mother giving all her love to the elder one. 'From the hour of my birth she hated me,' he wrote. 'Ours was not a united family.' To escape from such unhappiness, his father sent him to England for his education: to Rugby, then to Balliol College, Oxford, to which he claimed to have gained entrance by some judicious cheating in Latin Unseen. 'I hankered after oratory,' he wrote, and he practised public speaking in debates with G. K. Chesterton, W. B. Yeats and other visiting writers.

While still a schoolboy Collis had seen Bernard Shaw's political comedy *John Bull's Other Island* at the Abbey Theatre in Dublin. 'It was like hearing heavenly music – and I knew that at last I was feeling the real thing.' His first publication, 'a new book on an old subject', written in his early twenties, was simply called *Shaw*. Collis explains in his one-paragraph preface that 'some books are written for the pleasure of the reader and the profit of the writer, some for the profit of the reader and the pleasure of the writer, and some simply insist upon being written in spite of reader and writer ... [They] are often a great nuisance to the writer as well as to everybody else, but nevertheless they must be written. This is such a book.'

There is a sense of necessity in the writing, which Shaw could not help liking. Most biographers who wrote about G. B. S. during his lifetime had their pens taken from them so that he could rewrite many of their pages. But when Collis gave his chapters to Shaw, Shaw replied with letters, parts of which he allowed Collis to use as footnotes. They cover all sorts of subjects from vegetarian diets 'for poets and philosophers' to critics of Shakespeare from Voltaire to Dr Johnson (both quite different from Shaw's own criticism of Shakespearean bardolators such as Henry Irving). One footnote is a single word: 'Hooray!' It would make an interesting test to ask Shavian scholars what they thought Collis could have written to bring forth such a cheer. The sentence was: 'I fancy he has gained far more from listening to Wagner and Mozart than he has gained from all his reading put together.'

The Shaw who emerges from Collis's book is a man who conceals his generosity and is more often praised than understood by the public. He makes plenty of mistakes but often learns from them, and is a believer in evolution rather than revolution. The book was published in 1925 and was reprinted three times, gaining Collis some money to which he added £150 by selling his letters from Shaw. With this he soon set off abroad.

'Etna's volcano being in eruption I decided to go to Sicily at once and climb the mountain up to the crater if possible,' he later wrote in his autobiography *Bound Upon a Course* (1971). This book has its strengths and limitations. There are gaps in his own life, which were too painful to revisit at any length – in particular his unhappy childhood and apparently unfortunate first marriage.

He had married an American girl whom he had known for just one week. She believed he was a genius and would make a fortune. But he never did and she eventually decided he was a total failure. Meanwhile she became a medical pioneer with an intuitional flair for helping children with cerebral palsy. In the 1950s she herself was struck down with cerebral thrombosis. For six years Collis looked after her day and night – then for another six years she went into a nursing home – and one night she suddenly died. 'She had been dying slowly before my eyes for years,' he wrote. '... My friends thought it would be a release for me as well as for her ... I did not know my own heart. I did not know when the time came I would not be able to bear her *non-existence*.'

His marriage led him to study other people's marriages and come up with a new category of life-writing. 'Few of us know much about the married life even of our closest friends,' he wrote. 'Nothing is guarded so secretly as this matter. We do know something about the marriages of the famous whose lives have been documented by themselves and others. I have often thought that it is the same story as that of undocumented millions; the same story writ large.'

His three dual biographies cover the multiplicity of Strindberg's wives, the complexity of Tolstoy's marriage to Sonya and the charming courtship and discordant later life of Thomas and Jane Welsh Carlyle. The originality of these tight, swiftly

moving narratives with their ever-increasing drama did not
depend upon unpublished documents. He read all the published
correspondence, biographies and diaries he could find. Then he
reinterpreted what he had read. A good example of his ability to
merge comedy with tragedy comes from a famous photograph of
Tolstoy with his wife. It made an extraordinary impact on Collis.
This is what he wrote:

> September 23rd was the anniversary of their wedding. She was
> determined that a photograph should be taken of them together
> as a loving couple. He tried to get out of it, feeling embarrassed
> and ashamed. But she overruled all objections, and the photo-
> graph was taken... She was determined to make him turn his
> face towards her and smile. But he would not. He had often and
> often been deliberately gentle, with a loving word, or by giving
> her a pear, or by saying how pleased he was to see her eating
> pancakes – all duly noted in her diary. But not now. Here was a
> test (we never quite know when we are being tested) of the depth
> of his Christianity and the absoluteness of his cheek-turning
> principles. It would have been easy to have looked in her direc-
> tion and given her a smile. He would not... He looked to the
> front as hard as a cliff, and as obstinate. And there she stands, in
> her frightful clothes and her fierce possessive regard, and with
> a couple of handcuffs she has clapped upon him. And there he
> stands in the course blouse and the leather belt that he always
> wore ... a blind but unconquered Samson.

Despite his engaging life of Christopher Columbus (1976),
Collis was not a talented traveller. His adventurous journeys were
often less dramatic than the strolls he made round London and
described in *An Irishman's England* (1937). Earlier, when wearing gym shoes and carrying his satchel, he had climbed to the
very edge of Etna's erupting crater, he saw nothing except clouds
of sulphurous smoke. But travelling at rush hour by tube across
London he fell – not to the ground but into a crowd of passengers
that, as they swept along, held him at an angle of forty-five degrees.
'I have often wondered at the endurance of the people hanging

up there on their straps like dead animals ... they all insist upon coming home at the same moment, and hundreds who could go back by boat along the Thames in summer refuse to do so.' There was, he concluded, 'too little despair in this city... Therefore not enough hope. Only endurance.' The secret of London, he concluded, was the secret of beauty itself, which arises, like love and truth, 'out of the agony of the world'. It is not surprising that Robert Macfarlane believed that Collis belonged to the same literary family as another Irish writer: Samuel Beckett.

There is the orator's voice in much of Collis's writing. His description of travelling to Rotherhithe to buy a chair has something of Beckett's humour of desolation. After a good deal of waiting, the journey began.

> We arrived at Stepney – but not at our destination. We got into a bus: we got out of it. We got into a tram and out of it. We crossed streets and changed into more trams. We stood in the wind ... It was a cold and bloodless day, and at that hour of the afternoon when all meaning is withdrawn from the universe. And in the midst, our guide ... a timeless expression on her face. She was coming to help us buy this chair... she stood in the tram, waited by the kerb, walked through the alleys – wholly indifferent to the world ... Her figure assumed a gigantic shape ... the atlas of injustice.

An Irishman's England is dotted with short sentences as he reflects on diverse aspects of England between the two world wars. 'I once met a man walking up Charing Cross Road,' he wrote, 'accompanied by a small elephant.' Yet no one else seems to notice this. One windy day he takes cover and sees a bird-like woman blown 'in all the plumes of her sophistication, from Upper to Lower Regent Street'. He describes Marble Arch as 'a gateway leading nowhere' – perhaps a metaphor for the whole country.

In some fifteen books Collis focused on the 'extraordinary nature of the ordinary'. He was essentially a poet who studied the sciences, discovering the mysteries of what we take for granted.

'He was *sui generis*,' wrote A. N. Wilson, who as literary editor of the *Spectator* was 'happy to publish anything he wrote' towards the end of Collis's life. 'He survives in his books,' A. N. Wilson adds. But what would bring him alive for a new generation of readers would be an anthology of the best pages from these neglected publications.

The Many Lives of Frank Harris

Does anyone today know who Frank Harris was? Are his novels and biographies read at all now? A hundred years ago he was acknowledged 'by all great men of letters of his time to be ... greater than his contemporaries because he is a master of life', wrote the critic John Middleton Murry. George Meredith likened his novels to Balzac's, and Bernard Shaw his short stories to Maupassant – high praise that was somewhat deflated by the discovery that one story had been actually lifted from Stendhal. But no one would have been more astonished at his disappearance as a great man of letters than Frank Harris himself. 'Christ goes deeper than I do,' he explained, 'but I have had wider experience.'

I first heard of Frank Harris from the biographer Hesketh Pearson. When he was young he had praised Harris as being 'the most dynamic writer alive'. This praise diminished over the years and Pearson never wrote a life of Harris. But he made several comic appearances in my biographies. It was difficult to avoid him. There have been half-a-dozen published lives of him and he makes many appearances in other writers' autobiographies. He seems also to have inspired several characters in works of fiction. Ford Madox Ford presented him in *The Simple Life Limited* (1911) as George Everard, 'his horrible unique self'. In Frederic Carrel's novel *The Adventures of John Johns* (1879) there is a caricature of him becoming editor of a newspaper by seducing the proprietor's wife. In George and Weedon Grossmith's *The Diary of a Nobody* (1892) he has the name Hardfur Huttle, 'a man who did all the talking' and came out with the most alarming ideas.

H. G. Wells used him in his science-fiction novel *The War in the Air* (1908) as Butteridge, 'a man singularly free from false modesty' who believes 'all we have we owe to women'. It is surprising that a man with so many fictional lives seemed to disappear during the late twentieth century.

After his death, Harris came to life again in several dramatic roles. He appeared in the film *Cowboy*, adapted in 1958 from his *My Reminiscences as a Cowboy*; then, in 1978, he could be seen in a BBC television play called *Fearless Frank* by Leonard Rossiter; and later in Tom Stoppard's theatre play, *The Invention of Love*. His correspondence with Bernard Shaw was quietly published in 1982. Somehow and somewhere, his exploits were always available.

The 'connoisseur of Harris' was Hugh Kingsmill. In 1919 he published a novel called *The Will to Love*, which he had written in a prisoner-of-war camp. Harris appears in it as Ralph Parker, a man whose friendship 'was a craving for an audience, his love, lust in fancy dress'. Yet 'in the ruins of his nature, crushed but not extinct, something genuine and noble struggled to express itself'. Harris was in his seventies when he died in the summer of 1931 and Kingsmill's biography of him was published the following year. They had known each other for twenty years and the book was one of those lives that contain two main characters: the subject and the writer.

Kingsmill treats Harris as a comedian without a sense of humour. He seemed to be two different people, a Robin Hood who robbed the rich to help the poor – and was determined not to be poor himself. He jettisoned one belief for another, longing for many things he did not want. A born actor was what he appeared to be, someone whose best performance was playing the noble art of seduction. 'His praise of sensuality,' Kingsmill wrote, '... sounded melodiously in the ear of youth, and I hastened to sit at the feet of a master whose message agreed so well with what I desired from life.'

Harris's mother had died when he was aged three – and his sister was to instruct him how to attract girls and make a good marriage. Kingsmill described the rules as follows: 'First, praise the good points of the girl's face and figure; secondly, notice and approve her dress, for she will think you really like her if you notice her clothes; thirdly tell her she is unique ... and finally, kiss her.' To this Harris was to add 'the principle of feigned indifference'. He learnt all this so as to overcome his ugliness. 'I examined myself in a mirror, saw that I was ugly, and never looked at myself again.' His black hair was thick and low on his forehead, his features were irregular, he had large ears, an energetic chin and, worst of all, he was ridiculously short for a man of action. He tried to offset these disadvantages by developing his muscles until he resembled a prizefighter. To gain an extra inch in height he used elevators in his boots and to avoid overtaxing his digestion he made use of a stomach pump. His aim was to get pleasure and avoid its consequences – what Kingsmill described as 'to eat his cake and not have it'.

Harris did not understand that although men were attracted to women mainly by what they saw, women were more attracted to men by what they heard. Harris's attraction lay in his voice. He was endowed with a strong, dark, resonant, bass voice used with amazing fluency when he gave public speeches. To his young disciples he seemed the one man who could put the world to rights.

Frank, originally called James Thomas, had been born at one time or another during the 1850s, perhaps in Ireland, possibly in Wales – all depending on which of his autobiographical writings you read. Kingsmill did not hunt for certainties; he used Harris's escape from the storehouse of facts as a revelation of his character. 'He was born uneasy,' Kingsmill wrote. He hated his time at school, where he was bullied by bigger boys, and he did not get on well with his father. At the age of fourteen, with great courage and ingenuity, he set off for America to seek a happier life.

On reaching New York he became a bootblack, a workman in the caissons of Brooklyn Bridge and, arriving in Chicago, a night clerk at a hotel, where he joined a group of cowboys. Somehow his horsemanship enabled him to write on bullfighting with the knowledge of an expert. He spent some time at Kansas University studying law and did not return to Europe until his very early

twenties, travelling back by several routes. 'Harris travelling west-
wards across the Pacific and Harris travelling eastwards across the
Atlantic met again in Paris,' Kingsmill explained.

Back in Britain he was to become the editor of several newspapers and magazines, which gave him a prominent place in the
literary scene. He began editing the *Evening News*, giving readers
the suggestive and sensational stories he had enjoyed at the age
of fourteen. Kingsmill quotes some of his headlines: 'Mad Dogs
in the Metropolis', 'Measles in Church', 'Extraordinary Charge
against a Clergyman', 'Awful Death in a Brewery'. He had the
adroitness of a journalist and increased the sales of the papers he
edited – the *Fortnightly Review, Saturday Review* and *Modern
Society*. But 'his downfall was sudden and complete as his rise
had been brilliant and unexpected'. This was because he took no
notice of what the proprietors wanted. He became discontented at
reporting other people's happenings: he wanted to create happenings himself – especially political happenings. Adventures, he
decided, came to the adventurous. He set about becoming a Tory
Member of Parliament, marrying a wealthy widow who lived in
Park Lane and entertaining politicians and businessmen – only to
discover he thoroughly disliked them. He was a Tory, it is true,
but he was also a socialist and anarchist.

Kingsmill singled out three subjects of special interest among
the biographies Harris wrote: Bernard Shaw, Oscar Wilde and
Shakespeare. He wrote about Shaw at the end of his life and his
biography was published posthumously. According to Shaw,
Harris had 'an elaborate hypothesis of some fundamental weakness in my constitution' and it amused him to counteract this
with his generosity. Harris 'was grateful to Shaw for his unbroken
friendliness', Kingsmill wrote, '… yet resentful at being helped
by a man whose success exasperated him'. One of Shaw's most
generous acts was to contribute a chapter to Harris's life of Wilde.

Wilde had initially been repelled by Harris, while Harris was
impressed by Wilde's charm, humour and social success. It was
Harris who was to warn Wilde what would happen after Lord
Queensberry had been acquitted of criminal libel. He urged
Wilde to leave the country at once – a yacht was waiting for him

in the Thames. But Wilde seemed to have lost his nerve and was, as Harris predicted, found guilty of gross indecency and sent to jail for two years. Harris tried unsuccessfully to get well-known writers to sign a petition for his release and then visited Reading Gaol, where he succeeded in getting him more humane conditions. And then he ruined their friendship. He took the plot of a play Wilde had planned and made it his own. He promised him money when Wilde was out of prison – and never gave it to him. And Wilde, who had been in tears at Harris's kindness, came to the conclusion that he 'has no feelings. It is the secret of his success.' Yet Harris had been brave: defending Wilde to the extent that he had to insist he himself was not homosexual – though, he added thoughtfully 'if Shakespeare had asked me, I would have had to submit'.

Harris's *Oscar Wilde: His Life and Confessions* was published in 1916. *The Man Shakespeare and his Tragic Life Story* had come out after many years of writing and research seven years earlier. 'Frank Harris is upstairs,' Oscar Wilde had written, 'thinking about Shakespeare at the top of his voice.' It was probably his desire for fame that first prompted Harris to write about Shakespeare. On some pages he seems to confuse Shakespeare with himself. But his aim was to reveal the man behind the plays – the Victorians who studied the plays having forgotten there was such a man. He had read Georg Brandes's recent study of Shakespeare, which he described as 'the ablest of Shakespeare's commentaries' though, Kingsmill noted, he made 'no acknowledgement of his obvious debt to him'. Despite Harris's imperfections, Kingsmill's book ends with his strengths.

> The finest passage in his writings is where he passes in review the spokesmen of Shakespeare's sadness or despair: Richard II sounding the shallow vanity of man's desires, the futility of man's hopes; Brutus taking an everlasting farewell of his friend and going willingly to his rest; Hamlet desiring unsentient death; Vincentio turning to sleep from life's deceptions; Lear with his shrieks of pain and pitiful ravings; Macbeth crying from the outer darkness.

Kingsmill's biography is neither adulation nor an attack. Out of his candid recognition of weakness, Rebecca West wrote, 'there comes a living portrait which has made at least one reader who found Frank Harris's personality violently antipathetic understand why a great many people adored him and forgave him'.

Chinese Puzzles

In August 2001 I received an invitation from Peking University, Beijing (a rather odd combination of names, I thought) to speak at an international biography conference, which was to be held towards the end of the year at Fuzhou University – Fuzhou being the capital city of Fujian Province in south-east China. The letter was signed by the 'Director of the World Auto-Biography Center', Dr Zhao Baisheng, writing from the English department of Peking University.

I had been to China once before, in the summer of 1993, and was curious to see how things had changed over the last eight years. I was also interested to find out more of this universal centre of 'auto-biography'. So I replied saying that in principle I would be delighted to accept. There followed seven weeks of silence.

Suddenly, in late October, the silence was shattered by an artillery of emails, airmail letters and other messages. Originally I had been politely urged to ask any questions I wished: now I was the target for volleys of questions myself. What was my name, my title, my sex, my age, my profession, institution, nationality and so on? I felt somewhat disconcerted by all this, having assumed that my hosts knew who I was before inviting me to join them. Other questions, too, filled me with a vague dismay. How many people were accompanying me? What were my tour plans and flight numbers? Was I, by any chance, in need of accommodation – and if so what might it be? And then there was the minefield that lay between me and my visa. Among other documents, I would need a business letter in the United Kingdom confirming my financial responsibility, and another official letter stamped by a local municipal government or ministry of foreign affairs in China. I stared at this maze of 'information' with mounting helplessness. Then I sent off an SOS to the British Council.

Without the rapid and efficient assistance from the British Council offices in London, Beijing and Guangzhou, my visit to China would never have taken place. While they laboured over the bureaucracy of my journey, I worked at my 'keynote address', which, I was informed, would be translated before I arrived. I was advised to 'follow the MLA Style Manual' but this advice did not help me and would have been an extra encumbrance had I not decided to ignore it. Besides, there was very little time for such adornments: I was to email an abstract of my address at once, and forward my complete typescript as quickly as possible – preferably quicker. One night after grappling with this, I had a dream in which I stood before a large crowd in what looked like Tiananmen Square, and announced: 'My address is 85 St Mark's Road.' After immense applause I woke up.

My journey to Beijing was complicated. I flew first to Dublin, where I was one of the judges for the Impac Literary Award. From Dublin I flew back to Heathrow, from Heathrow to Paris, and then on to Beijing. Though one of these flights was cancelled, another was sufficiently delayed for me to make the connection, and I arrived in Beijing in time for lunch instead of breakfast.

On my first visit to China I had travelled with Doris Lessing and my wife, Margaret Drabble. This was, to a large extent, a VIP trip, hosted by the Chinese Writers' Association and involving translators, editors of magazines and publishing houses. We were interviewed on television and in newspapers, and we made presentations of our books to universities – at least Doris and Maggie did. My books never arrived. This is a problem I have encountered in several countries, a problem that afflicts non-fiction writers, whose works are shelved not under their names but under the names of their subjects. Look under H and there is no sighting my lives of Strachey or Shaw. I recommend travelling biographers to choose subjects whose names have at least an opening syllable identical to their own. To set an example I am contemplating a life of Richard Holmes. By the end of our 1993 visit, though I shared the platform with Doris and Maggie as we attempted to describe the various aspects of contemporary British literature, my bookless condition had convinced the Chinese authorities that I was no author but a government official, perhaps from the celebrated Scotland Yard, appointed to keep an eye on these wild lady novelists. I was not particularly convincing, rising to my feet at the conclusion of various lunches and dinners after an embarrassing performance with my chopsticks, my clothes littered with delicious fish, meat and vegetables, to make a final speech of thanks on behalf of the three of us, only to find as I sat down that the banquet was far from over – another soup was on its way.

During that early visit we were escorted everywhere – to the Forbidden City, the Beijing Opera, the Great Wall, the Buried City of Xi'an, the Shanghai Academy of Social Science – by a brilliant young translator. She was especially eager to meet the director of the films *Red Sorghum* and *Raise the Red Lantern*, Zhang Yimou, whom we had asked to meet.

But this second visit was different. I was on my own, free to walk wherever I wished. I was surprised by what I saw. There is a popular notion in the West that the Chinese are censored and inscrutable. But in the towns I found the very opposite: the streets were full of vivacious crowds, some of them singing as they bicycled fluently through the dense traffic, many of them joined in laughter. Even some political jokes are allowed. The huge figure of Chairman Mao, as big as a Buddha, with one hand outstretched, his fingers clearly separated, is insisting, it is said, on a five-day working week.

One change that particularly struck me were the groups of young men and women flirting, kissing, arms round each other in the streets and parks. Feminism is coming to China and it will, I believe, affect the 'Little Emperor' problem – the law which restricts every family to one child. You can see these single children everywhere, dressed in wonderfully coloured clothes – each one a little emperor or empress. This is less the case in the countryside, where the law is more difficult to administer. But soon women will no longer tolerate this law. They will win the day [the law was changed a couple of years later].

There are the same herds of bicycles in Beijing, but more cars now. And more buildings are going up, often banks, hotels and offices. It is not so modern a place as Shanghai (which is scheduled to take over from Hong Kong as the chief trading centre), but from a distance Beijing begins to look like any large American city. Some older blocks of flats will be taken down as the Olympic Games approaches and people moved elsewhere – to better accommodation perhaps, but in districts where they may not want to live. Money rules – as it does here and in the United States. The news that China is entering the World Trade Organisation is greeted as a great step forward. All the experts proclaim this on television and in the newspapers. But the strength of the Chinese economy is growing dramatically, while other countries fall towards recession – partly because of its low wages. The government is rich: most of the people are not.

On my first visit I found some people openly discussing the Cultural Revolution: its valid beginnings, its terrible excesses. One evening I had dinner with a father and son, one who had been imprisoned at that time, the other who had joined the marauding Red Guards. They had come through all this and spoke about their experiences with amiability and sophistication, their fundamental belief in communism undented.

All of us were advised in 1993 not to mention Tibet. It is not a subject like Northern Ireland that could be freely debated. The official view is that Tibet had fallen into terrible backwardness and poverty, and needed to be liberated by China and brought up to date. The media was filled with news, while I was there, of a large exhibition of Tibetan culture then showing in Australia. I could not detect any sense of irony in the reporting of this exhibition.

The other unmentionable T word was Taiwan. So I mentioned it. Rather to my surprise I discovered that there had been some trade between Taiwan and the mainland. People nearby, living on the south-east coast of China, I was told, can speak to their families on the island using mobile phones. The independence of Taiwan is not generally felt to be a very vital issue, and I sensed a feeling that it will one day be part of China again. What the authorities dislike is foreign interference, and the placing of such matters on the world's political agenda – particularly on the agenda of the United States. This is felt to be an insult to the Chinese nation – and suddenly the military presence, which for the most part is out of sight, makes a sinister appearance.

One day, losing my way in Beijing, I came across some soldiers idling and then drilling on a parade ground. I watched carefully. They seemed to me like the security officials at airports – unsmiling, dour, with faces like machines and quite unlike the active, vocal taxi drivers and shopkeepers. To my eyes they had the wooden appearance of people who are underemployed and would welcome a little more action.

Another day I saw on television an interview-confession of a woman who had been sentenced to three years' imprisonment for being a member of the religious cult Falun Gong. She had been tempted into this 'alternative' way of life while living in the United States. What she had done wrong was unclear to me. But the confession itself was a most sophisticated affair, admitting the attractions of this belief but condemning its self-destructive excesses. Religion, it seems, is fine when seen as part of the past – and part of the tourist trade. But any supernatural philosophy is still regarded as a potential threat. The woman interviewed was attractive and well dressed – almost an advertisement for Chinese prison life. But it showed how much, and then how little, may be tolerated in China.

The United States is not very popular in China – any more than Islam. Americans are constantly being told by their ungodly politicians that the United States is God's Own Country. The haute cuisine of McDonald's and the celluloid violence of Hollywood are not always good ambassadors. There seems to be a lack of subtlety in this exported culture. Like the paradoxical 'war to end wars', the terror to end terrors continually sows more terror around us.

And yet China needs the United States. It must sup with the devil because he is so damn wealthy. Many Chinese students would like to go there and be rich themselves. There are more students studying international business, computer skills and the magic realism of the virtual world than studying literature and the arts. The teaching sometimes reflects the authoritarian nature of the country: the professors profess, the students, like secretaries, accept dictation, and there seems little live dialogue between them. On my first visit I had asked the students to write down any questions they wanted to ask while I was speaking – to avoid their shyness in getting up and questioning me in a foreign language. But when lecturing in Peking University this time, I omitted to do this, and so had to initiate a dialogue by asking them some questions. Did they write diaries and let anyone else read them? Did they keep letters they were sent – or was it all fax and email now? They responded eagerly and I discovered that more than one student kept two diaries: one to be shown to others (including sometimes their parents), the other strictly for herself. This seemed to me to reflect the dual nature of Chinese society very neatly.

The international conference itself – reached by a seven-hour hectically crowded train journey and then a coach trip through the night – was an extraordinary event. A large contingent of American scholars had been invited and had been keen to sign in for it. But that was by the first week of September. Following the coordinated terrorist attacks on 11 September, they began to cancel. By early November only five of them remained. But this gang of five then cancelled because the others were not coming.

Where the Americans led, others followed and stayed at home. I was left as the only participant who actually flew in from abroad, though various foreign scholars who already had teaching posts in China were drafted in to fill some gaps. The conference suddenly covered Arabic, Russian and Latin American literature

As the innocent one from abroad, I was overwhelmed with gratitude and flattery. It was an intimidating experience. I found myself without a translator, giving the opening speech to an audience of some 400 students and scholars in a magnificent, tent-like auditorium; and then, a little later on the eighth floor of a hotel, co-chairing a seminar on language acquisition, the interplay of fact and fiction in the novels of Jeanette Winterson, and the overlapping of pathology, eulogy and autobiography in the non-fiction work of the Australian poet Peter Rose.

Almost everything took me by surprise. For example, the 'Round-table Session' was conducted from twelve bamboo gondolas skimming along a river in the dramatic landscape of Wuyi Mountain; and the 'Global Perspectives' session seemed to take place in a nightclub with much singing and dancing. I remember, years ago at a festival in New Zealand, being told by Kazuo Ishiguro that, in the interests of furthering my career, I should become more like Mick Jagger. If only I could have done this, how I might have shone at Global Perspectives.

It was English pragmatism, I discovered, rather than English irony that most amuses the Chinese. My agitation on finding I was booked on a plane that did not exist added greatly to the jollity of the conference. What else was this but a devastating politeness, indicating their wish to see me stay for ever in China?

Nietzsche Contra Shaw

'The difficulty now is to get rid of me,' Friedrich Nietzsche wrote to his friend Georg Brandes in the late 1880s. And Shaw would have agreed. In Shavian style he liked to use Nietzsche's name but to distance himself from the one or two translations of Nietzsche's books he had read.

After writing his 'comedy and philosophy' *Man and Superman* early in the twentieth century, Shaw was assumed by a number of critics, including his friend William Archer and also G. K. Chesterton, to be a disciple of Nietzsche. It is true that in his letters and prefaces he was using Nietzsche's name quite freely. He did so partly because he believed that British culture was becoming too backward and inward-looking. To change this internal focus he championed what was new and foreign in philosophy and the arts. In his art criticism he praised Whistler; in his theatre criticism he blew the trumpet for Ibsen, Chekhov and later Strindberg. And he devoted much of his music criticism to Wagner, with whom Nietzsche had quarrelled.

Shaw enjoyed making lists of American, Scandinavian, German and Russian writers. In the preface to *Man and Superman* he introduces readers to a series of authors whose thinking could be taken as somewhat similar to his own: 'Goethe, Shelley, Schopenhauer, Wagner, Ibsen, Morris, Tolstoy and Nietzsche.'

We do not think of Shaw being heavily influenced by Tolstoy, Goethe (who also used the Superman for Faust) or Shelley. But Nietzsche's name has stuck to him partly because he used the word Superman, a translation of Nietzsche's Übermensch from *Thus*

Spake Zarathustra. It was a 'good cry' he thought – which was to say a good piece of advertising that would contribute nicely to the title of his new 'comedy and philosophy' for the stage.

People read Nietzsche for his philosophy; they go to Shaw's plays for their comedy. In the philosophical dream sequence in *Man and Superman* Shaw mentions Nietzsche as having found himself in hell. The Devil, who represents Shaw's hidden pessimism and speaks in Shavian parodies, believes Nietzsche's loss of 'wits' during his final years on earth had been inevitable. His career became a cautionary tale. He had been led into pessimism by a lifetime of searching for an optimistic philosophy while ignoring the lessons that human nature and human history could have taught him. But after a period in Shaw's hell, he regains his wits, his confidence, and takes the escalator up to heaven as if he were happily entering a university again. After which we hear no more of him.

This short, somewhat misleading, discussion by the Devil about Nietzsche in the dream scene was cut from the recent [2015] production of *Man and Superman* at the National Theatre, with the result that there is very little to connect Nietzsche and Shaw. It is a hundred years since the play was first produced in its prodigious entirety and cuts were essential – a reading of it all took over five hours. Nietzsche lived 'Beyond Space, Beyond Time', very far from Shaw's world. In contemporary political life, Shaw was a committed socialist who, in the early twentieth century, gave £1,000 (equivalent to £50,000 today) to help start the *New Statesman* and also bought shares, becoming one of its original proprietors and directors. 'I won't write,' he promised. But he could not help himself and soon became a prolific contributor to the paper – in none of whose contributions is there a mention of Nietzsche.

What, then, did Shaw admire in Nietzsche? In the absence of God, both of them were seeking a purpose. There was Nietzsche's belief in struggle, which Shaw acknowledged as necessary for essential improvement; there was also his attack on traditional moral values, which acted as a brake on necessary change. He was clever and imaginative and sometimes original. But Shaw was not one of Nietzsche's 'brethren' who is urged to see 'the rainbow and the bridges of the Superman'.

The first of Shaw's writings said to have been influenced by Nietzsche was *The Quintessence of Ibsenism*. But this was written at the beginning of the 1890s, before he had read any Nietzsche. In 1896 he read *Nietzsche Contra Wagner*, translated by Thomas Common, and reviewed it in *The Saturday Review*. His review paints an unattractive pen portrait of Nietzsche, certainly not of someone who would become a great influence on his thinking. 'Such a philosopher is as dull and dry as you please: it is he who brings his profession into disrepute,' Shaw wrote. '...Nietzsche is the champion of privilege, of power and of inequality.' He described his philosophy as a 'fictitious hypothesis', by which he meant that nothing came to him as the result of actual experience. It was all put together by 'a mere dead piece of brain machinery ... Never was there a deafer, blinder, socially and politically inepter academician.'

There were obvious differences between the two writers. Nietzsche was an academic; Shaw never went to a university. Nietzsche, it seems, came to believe in the usefulness of war, while Shaw was continually trying to take power away from men with guns and hand it to men and women of imagination and intellect. Nietzsche believed that 'convictions are prisons' while Shaw gloried in his convictions – one of them being his belief in the equality of income. He pointed to 'suggestive combinations of ideas' that were 'pregnant with vitality' in Nietzsche's writings. But many of these sallies seemed 'petulant and impossible' and his epigrams appeared to have been 'written with phosphorus on brimstone'. Some critics may see the well-known epigram in *Human, All Too Human* – 'a joke is an epigram on the death of a feeling' – as tailor-made for G. B. S. with his many jokes and his apparent poverty of emotion. But Shaw himself maintained that an essential ingredient of truth was humour.

'I must really read some of his stuff,' Shaw teased William Archer soon after the publication of *Man and Superman*. But the more he learnt about Nietzsche the more disapproval he felt for what would be his growing authority on modern literary

criticism. 'Not for a moment will I suffer anyone to compare me
to him as a critic,' he concluded. In a letter to his American biographer Archibald Henderson some four months after *Man and
Superman* had opened at the Court Theatre in London, he wrote
that 'Nietzsche's notions of art, his admiration of the Romans &c,
are very unlike any view of mine ... and his erudition I believe to
be all nonsense: I think he was an academic in the sense of having
a great deal of secondhand booklearning about him...'

Whereas Shaw travelled widely and was seen as a public and
political figure, Nietzsche nursed his genius in a hothouse, creating powerful and passionate ideas that were remote from ordinary
life outside. Brought up with a clerical background, he had no
belief in Christianity, which he considered a trick that disarmed
people of the courage they needed to deal with the suffering in
life. He could gain no comfort himself from any religion. But
with God dead, what was the purpose of human beings? Were
they part of an unknown experiment or was everything mean-
ingless? He saw the possibility of men and women retreating into
animals. Or might they progress in positive ways that he could
inspire, transforming them into superhumans and taking the place
of gods? Nietzschean philosophers have made ingenious attempts
to reassemble his queries and contradictions into an equation
pointing to a solution that removes meaning from intention and
changes even nihilism into a positive doctrine.

Shaw's hope lay in the children of mixed marriages and, in *Back
to Methuselah,* an ever-longer span of life, changing our focus
on what is necessary and desirable. He believed in the life ever-
lasting – but not necessarily for the individual. When he looked
back on our history he was overtaken by a dark pessimism that
animated the speeches of the Devil in *Man and Superman*. But
when Nietzsche looked back, he saw some hope in the Roman
Empire, suggesting that slavery was a necessity for a mentally
aristocratic life. 'Men shall be trained for war,' he wrote, 'and
woman for the recreation of the warrior.' Shaw believed that
women should have as many children as they wanted – but each
one preferably by a different man so we could break through
our social and tribal barriers. When Nietzsche looked into the

future and beyond the sinking sun he imagined a paradise full of light and logic, a distant Utopia of which he was the prophet. Within universities Nietzsche's language is peculiarly stimulating, the word warfare meaning little more than a tense intellectual debate. But carry that language into the streets and it becomes dangerously aggressive. Early in 1889, shortly before the birth of Hitler, Nietzsche went mad.

What Shaw may have envied was Nietzsche's posthumous fame and authority. Occasionally he would call himself a Nietzschean, but this can be taken too literally. For example, he wrote to his German translator Siegfried Trebitsch while at work on *Man and Superman*: 'I want the Germans to know me as a philosopher; as an English (or Irish) Nietzsche (only ten times cleverer).'

In his prefaces and essays Shaw crowded his pages with writers' names to show he was no solitary eccentric, but part of an international zeitgeist. The poets, playwrights and philosophers he refers to are mostly attempting to solve a similar problem of how to advance human beings to the next stage of evolution. None of them necessarily influenced the other, but all of them were working along roughly parallel lines to discover an individual answer to a general question – as Charles Darwin and Alfred Russel Wallace had done.

The latest edition of *The Oxford Companion to English Literature* assembles some diverse literary figures, including Shaw, who 'felt the impact of Nietzsche's thought'. In a similar vein the distinguished Nietzsche scholar Keith Ansell-Pearson has suggested that Shaw was one of the writers who were 'avid readers of Nietzsche' and 'inspired by his ideas'. But having seen Act III of *Man and Superman* at the National Theatre, he concluded that this was not a version of Nietzsche but much closer to the *Creative Evolution* of Henri Bergson. And Shaw himself would have endorsed this. For though insisting that Bergson's and his writings were 'totally independent of one another', he added that his scene in hell turned out to be 'a dramatisation' of Bergson's philosophy.

There are no characters in Shaw's plays that have their origins in Nietzsche's 'self-effacing self-advancement'. But something of

Nietzsche's spirit and powerful influence can perhaps be detected in part of *Geneva,* Shaw's political extravaganza written in the late 1930s. Here the European dictators – Bardo Bombardone of Italy, Ernest Battler of Germany and General Flanco de Fortinbras of Spain – are summoned to the Court of International Justice at The Hague. It is the bumptious actor-politician Bardo Bombardone (much admired at that time by Battler) who delivers a flight of words in praise of willpower and war. This is a doctrine that, forty years after his death, might have been familiar to Nietzsche – if only as a parody. 'My time has not yet come,' he had written in *Ecce Homo,* 'some are born posthumously.' But a pantomime version of Mussolini in Shaw's theatrical extravaganza was far from the posthumous destination of Nietzsche's dreams.

Shaw himself was to choose a very different modern Superman, a genius belonging to another order of influential men, a far-seeing realist who changed our understanding of the world, giving us a new focus on time and the future: Einstein. 'I rejoice at the new universe to which he has introduced us,' Shaw declared. 'I rejoice in the fact that he has destroyed all our old sermons, all the old absolutes, all the old cut and dried conceptions, even of time and space, which were so discouraging.' But neither Shaw nor Nietzsche could have foreseen the reinvention today of so many gods, all armed with their warring sermons and absolutes.

The Politics of Polonius

'Neither a borrower nor a lender be.' This was a phrase I remember my grandfather using years ago. As a child I did not know that it came from *Hamlet* and was spoken by Polonius, that 'tedious old fool' who traded in clichés and possessed an unsuspected genius for enabling tragedy.

A good deal of borrowing and lending went on among the gentry in Shakespeare's time and Polonius's sententious advice to his son Laertes, as he sails for Paris to complete his education as a gentleman, must have raised some ironic smiles among audiences. Shakespeare scholars have debated among themselves as to whether Polonius, being chief minister to King Claudius, might have been based on William Cecil (Baron Burghley), who was Queen Elizabeth's chief minister. But what interests me is the fact that we can see versions of Polonius crowding round prime ministers and their cabinets in our own time. It is they who draft the speeches for party conferences.

Margaret Thatcher compared her job as prime minister to the head of a family who looked after the household. She treated the country as if it were a large family unit that belonged to her and was careful not to spoil us. She had to balance the country's accounts and pay off its debts, she reminded us, as responsible families balanced their own accounts. We were, in effect, being treated to Polonius's guidance on husbandry, with Mrs Thatcher starring as the exemplary housewife.

Although Attlee turned his back on public appearances and Heath was never happy in the limelight, more recent prime ministers have breathed in publicity ever more deeply, nourishing their careers as if with an elixir. They are the leaders of our tedious celebrity culture and are themselves led by the camera and the microphone, seeking photo opportunities anywhere and every-where – at cricket matches and schools, on building sites, in tents of soldiers and by hospital beds. They cannot resist intruding into criminal trials, athletic events, royal happenings and the deaths of famous people they never knew, walking among us as Polonius walked among the actors, speaking with good accents and good discretion (though without much content) and confusing popu-larity with democracy. They seem strangely unaware of how soon we grow sickened and exasperated by their devious attempts to please us. And so we vote them out. 'I took thee for thy better,' Hamlet says over Polonius's dead body.

Polonius was unable to follow his own advice, often giving tongue to what he himself called 'unproportioned thought' and self-important rhetoric. He was a windbag and a busybody who did not discover that being 'too busy is some danger'. Far from being true to himself, his political manoeuvrings at court put him in the service of a murderer, as he connived with the king to spy on Hamlet in order to advance himself. Such unproportioned thought comes naturally to our own politicians. We heard it when Gordon Brown famously declared that, as the result of his financial manage-ment, the days of boom-and-bust were finally at an end. We heard it again in Tony Blair's wishful thinking as he warned us how Saddam Hussein could send his devastating weapons into Britain within forty minutes. Blair and Bush started their 'war on terror' by trying to manufacture terror within us (that is the only sense that can be made of the phrase). They appeared to eliminate the past – the Great Depression of the 1930s, the fact that Saddam Hussein had been our ally, the retreat of the Soviet army from Afghanistan – and replace all this sombre reality with adventurous and lethal fantasies. Better in general to avoid interfering in civil wars – even in Libya. All countries, as part of their history, must be allowed their civil wars with no more than medical intervention from abroad.

I was brought up to mind my own business and to believe in the good sense of saving a proportion of my money. My father introduced me to his bank in the early 1950s and I am reminded of it whenever I see *Dad's Army* on television and hear the words of Captain Mainwaring, the local bank manager at Walmington-on-Sea. Those were simple, straightforward days. We trusted our banks – there was no question of them 'failing'. Indeed the verb 'to bank' meant the same as 'to save'.

It is all borrowing and lending now. No politician dares to speak against saving money – they simply make it very difficult. The Treasury's National Savings and Investment products have been severely reduced and rationed. Premium Bonds send out smaller cheques and the interest on NS&I direct ISAs are kept lower than those available at banks and building societies. Easy Access Accounts have been closed and put, alongside Pensioners' Guaranteed Income Bonds and Capital Bonds, in the dustbin. At the time of writing, no Savings Certificates are available.

What has taken the place of savings has been the inflation of house prices that are not calculated as part of inflation and give us a sense of being richer than we actually are. We must not save as my grandfather attempted to do, we must not budget as Mrs Thatcher believed we should and we cannot follow Polonius's advice any more than he could. Those who hoard the past and do not invest in or gamble on the future are likened to the man who buried his one talent in the ground and had no interest to show God the Banker on the day of reckoning. We must spend, even to the extreme of impoverishing ourselves, so that the country may be rich and the Treasury pocket more of our money as it circulates happily round and about us.

Capitalism is the most ingenious and seductive of all economic dreams. It is a Utopia that introduces us to something we had never thought possible: the ability to borrow from the future to pay for everything we want. We have done this in the belief that we would never reach that future but exist eternally in the present. Now we have woken from our dream and can see a country made barren and infertile under the accumulation of our debts. We have reached a wasteland of our own making. 'The rest is silence,' says Hamlet at the end of Shakespeare's tragedy. It is in the silence of our politicians, the words they do not speak, that we learn the truth.

Controversial Confessions

The Examined Life: How we Lose and Find Ourselves by Stephen Grosz

Stephen Grosz is a psychoanalyst who has worked in the United States and Britain. Over his career he has been 'sitting with patients for thousands of hours', he writes. Occasionally he has used his notes and observations for addresses at clinical seminars or for contributions to psychoanalytical journals. But this is the first time he has consulted his files in order to publish a book for the general reader.

'This book is about change,' he tells us. His troubled patients are seeking change, though they sometimes shield themselves from his professional intrusiveness. There is the risk, too, of change being for the worse – for the consultant as well as for the patient. These sessions are a learning process for both of them. Some of the most sympathetic passages in the book chronicle moments of the author's disquiet when he is left with a sense of 'failing both my patients and myself', or when he is confronted by someone who is irrevocably damaged.

For British readers there is the occasional off-putting Americanism such as 'different than' in place of 'different from' and the assumption that everyone has a childlike 'mom' and no one has an adult mother. But Stephen Grosz is an able writer, engaging, frank and with many penetrating insights. His short, succinct chapters have both the tension and the satisfaction of miniature detective or mystery stories. We are introduced to people telling blatant yet self-revealing lies, shown extraordinary everyday happenings, ingenious acts of transference and surreal episodes, such as the woman who, invited to lunch at someone's home, arrived with a 'removal van containing all her clothes and possessions, including some large pieces of furniture'.

Grosz invites his readers into his consulting room as a silent and invisible audience. So we also learn what he has learnt: that achieving success often involves loss; that people like to use boredom as a form of aggression; that the eager promotion of self-esteem in children may well lead to laziness; that silence is valuable and can be interpreted; and that the only real time is the present ('the past is alive in the present ... The future is not some place we're going to, but an idea in our mind now').

Anxiety, anger, loneliness, lovesickness, the fear of failure, separation and the sense of not being heard are some of the conditions that lead people to his consulting room. Stephen Grosz listens: therefore he is. But who is he? The reader is introduced to him in his two pages of acknowledgements at the end of this book. These pages are crowded with more than seventy people, including three generations of his family, considerable members of staff at his literary agency and publishers in several countries, also journalists and other writers, many colleagues in hospitals, clinics, institutions, universities and units. The impression is that he is never lonely, separated, lovesick, unseen or unheard. These acknowledgements are by way of being a professional CV testifying to his well-being and success.

Towards the end of their careers and in the event of their sudden death, psychoanalysts usually designate another member of their profession to 'dispose of any confidential notes or correspondence', Grosz explains. Although the identities of his patients are concealed and some details changed in this book, the essence of his confidential notes will already have been published by the time the originals come to be destroyed.

The situation is in some ways similar to that which surrounded Diane Middlebrook's biography of the American confessional poet Anne Sexton in 1991. Middlebrook asked Sexton's psychiatrist for her confidential tapes and was given them because the family wanted the nature of Sexton's infidelity, incest and the alcoholism that led to her suicide to be understood by the public. At the time this was considered a controversial arrangement that in no sense created a precedent. Has Stephen Grosz asked permission from his patients? After all, some of them, reading this book, may well recognise themselves. At the end of his acknowledgements Grosz writes that his 'greatest debt, finally, is to those who cannot be thanked by name – the patients whose lives have shaped this book'. These are his last words and they leave us with an unanswered question.

PART THREE

The Whispering Gallery

'… do you think it would be right to put Sir Allen
Lane in the dock, to charge him personally?'
Mervyn Griffith-Jones in
The Trial of Lady Chatterley by C. H. Rolph

INTRODUCTION

The Whispering Gallery was an audacious hoax published
anonymously between the two world wars. The book immediately became a bestseller, but its publishers were savagely attacked
by the *Daily Mail* and the dispute led to a famous trial in which
the author was defended by Sir Patrick Hastings, the Attorney
General. The reputations of many people were at stake, from
the Prince of Wales (Edward VIII) and Cecil Rhodes to Lord
Randolph Churchill and King Alfonso of Spain. The argument
was as to whether there was justice and morality in mixing invention and fact, what Virginia Woolf was to call the 'marriage of
granite and rainbow'. The debate may be seen as an experiment
bringing together the frontiers of biography and the novel to
create the highly controversial branch of contemporary literature
that now flourishes.

I met the author of *The Whispering Gallery* in the 1960s and he
told me the story of this trial.

DRAMATIS PERSONAE

Hesketh Pearson: an actor and journalist aged forty. He is a man of considerable charm who later became a well-known biographer.

Gladys Pearson: his sensible, loving wife aged thirty-five.

Allen Lane: The ambitious new managing director of the Bodley Head publishing company, in his mid-twenties. Later famous for creating Penguin Books and publishing the unexpurgated edition of *Lady Chatterley's Lover* in 1960.

Diana Pollen: A far-sighted senior editor at the Bodley Head. She is approximately sixty.

Sir Patrick Hastings: The new Attorney General, in his late forties. He had been knighted in 1924.

Sir Henry Curtis Bennett: a formidable barrister and Conservative politician. He is nearing fifty.

The voices of politicians in Scene One have been recorded by members of the cast.

The action takes place in London during 1926 and 1927.

SCENE ONE

A room in HESKETH *and* GLADYS *Pearson's apartment in London. On the sideboard stands a trumpet-shaped machine like that of the HMV brand image with a dog.* HESKETH *is sitting at his desk tinkering with this intricate device. The scene brings to mind* Krapp's Last Tape. *There is equipment to capture voices near the desk reminiscent of the phonograph and tiny organ pipes that decorate Professor Higgins's laboratory in Act Two of* Pygmalion.

HESKETH. Come along, Gladys. It's all ready.

GLADYS *speaks from the next room.*

GLADYS'S VOICE. Are you sure?

GLADYS *enters the room and goes to the sideboard as* HESKETH *continues tinkering with his machine.*

GLADYS. Hesketh! Did you hear me?

HESKETH. Of course I did. I always do. And yes I *am* sure. We'd better get on with it.

GLADYS. I didn't mean that.

There are signs of a slight irritation between them.

HESKETH. Well, what *did* you mean, then? We must give it a try.

GLADYS. Are you really going ahead with this scheme of yours? I can't help feeling it'll land us in trouble.

HESKETH. You worry too much. It'll be fun. And it should bring us in some money. We'll have a better life.

GLADYS. We have a good life now.

HESKETH. We do and we don't. But I'm fed up with being away half the year, going from one theatre to another all the time.

HESKETH *gets up and goes to* GLADYS. *He puts his hands on her shoulders.*

HESKETH. I'm away from you so much. I've had enough of it.

GLADYS *is obviously pleased.*

GLADYS. You *are* away a lot. But you love the theatre. You always have.

HESKETH. It's the *plays* I can't stand. I'm never in Shakespeare, never in Shaw. I'm in Ethel M. Dell, God help me. Do you remember those last words I had to speak at the end of that play of hers? What was it called?

GLADYS *is smiling. She knows what* HESKETH *is going to say.*

GLADYS. It was called *The Way of an Eagle.* I remember it well.

HESKETH. I wish *I* didn't. The worst of it was being left on stage as the curtain came down and delivering my last line.

HESKETH *goes to the front of the stage and with an exaggerated gesture delivers the awful lines.*

HESKETH. It is not the way of an eagle to sweep twice!

GLADYS *laughs and with mock innocence asks a question.*

GLADYS. Was that the time when someone in the audience shouted out: 'Shows what a bloody lot you know about eagles'?

HESKETH. Thank you for reminding me. I must get away from such things.

GLADYS. I still don't see why you are writing such a peculiar book …

HESKETH. You're right. It *is* a peculiar book – but all the better for that. Memoirs nowadays are unbelievably dull. They're so polite, so respectable, so bloody awful!

GLADYS. That's why I read novels.

HESKETH, *getting excited, begins walking up and down as he explains his plan.*

HESKETH. That's just my point. I want to show what people *really* think and feel. That's what novelists do. Have you heard of anything more negative than '*non*-fiction'? It's non-readable and written by nonentities.

GLADYS *is looking more worried as he speaks.*

GLADYS. That's all very well. But you must be careful or…

HESKETH. Or what? I'm sick of being careful. Everyone's careful these days. I want to take some risks…

GLADYS. *What* risks? That's what I want to know.

HESKETH *stops walking, faces* GLADYS, *and talks seriously to her.*

HESKETH. I don't mean invasions into people's love affairs – that's their own business. I mean uncovering their ambitions in public life. I want to use my instinct as well as my research. I'm having fun with this book.

GLADYS. I'm sure you are. But not everything is fun. If you don't look out it may end in tragedy.

HESKETH *comes slowly towards* GLADYS.

HESKETH. I don't see why. That's the last thing I want. Everything is changing and I want to be part of that change. That's all.

GLADYS *sympathetically comes close to* HESKETH.

GLADYS. I don't want to discourage you. I want to protect you. But I don't see why on earth you need to make recordings of what you've invented.

HESKETH. I'll tell you why. For years I've been listening to all sorts of famous people: politicians, newspaper tycoons, empty-headed celebrities, and have had to write down whatever they said, however idiotic. Now it's time to write what they *really* think and feel but dare not say.

GLADYS *looks perplexed.*

GLADYS. Books aren't normally written like that.

HESKETH *goes to the recording equipment and touches it as if it were his friend.*

HESKETH. I have to do it like this. I have an actor's ear. I can tell if it's authentic when I hear it. Do please help me. You've got a line in it yourself, remember.

GLADYS *smiles and joins him at the equipment.*

GLADYS. Of course I'll help. There's can't be any harm in listening to it. Tell me what happens before I say my sentence.

HESKETH *gives* GLADYS *a hug and begins speaking with enthusiasm.*

HESKETH. The scene opens one evening at 10 Downing Street. The ladies have left the dinner table and we hear the men chatting. It begins with Asquith, the prime minister, speaking to David Lloyd George. Then a bit later Winston Churchill joins in. It all takes place about ten years ago – early in 1916. Let's see how it goes.

HESKETH *and* GLADYS *fiddle with the sound machines and suddenly the room is filled with crackling and then the sound of the actors' voices pretending to be Asquith, David Lloyd George and Winston Churchill.*

ASQUITH. Now the ladies have gone we can speak more freely. I am expecting great news tonight.

LLOYD GEORGE. You are always expecting great news, Prime Minister.

HESKETH *is enjoying himself, and begins walking up and down and miming on stage what the politicians are saying.* GLADYS *watches him with amusement.*

ASQUITH. Things are moving at last.

LLOYD GEORGE. I'm sure they are – moving backwards is my guess.

CHURCHILL. Let's wait and see.

LLOYD GEORGE. People think we are winning the war because of Kitchener, Winston. I think we're losing it because of him.

ASQUITH. You're jealous of Kitchener. But he is a big man...

LLOYD GEORGE. Six foot two, I believe.

ASQUITH. Very funny, David. But he's a patriot. Without Kitchener we would never have had an army worth the name – and none of us would have remained in office for a week.

CHURCHILL. Oh come now, Prime Minister. How do you make that out?

ASQUITH. As you very well know, Winston, whenever there's a war the country turns instinctively to the Conservative Party. We Liberals gave them Kitchener and saved our own skins by doing so.

We hear a knock at the door and GLADYS's *voice.* HESKETH *points to* GLADYS *and she smiles back at him.*

GLADYS'S VOICE. You are wanted on the telephone, Prime Minister.

HESKETH, *who has been listening with intense animation, switches off the recording and turns to* GLADYS, *speaking hopefully.*

HESKETH. So what do you think, Glad? It's fun, isn't it?

GLADYS. I can see that it's given *you* a lot of fun. But I'm still muddled. There are things I want to know.

HESKETH. What things?

GLADYS. I want to know what's supposed to be happening.

HESKETH. Asquith had appointed Kitchener as secretary of state for war. But the war was going badly and people were blaming him for the setbacks. Later in 1916 Lloyd George will replace Asquith as prime minister. So there's a lot about to happen.

GLADYS. What about Churchill?

HESKETH. Churchill loves war. It excites him. He cannot help himself. But he doesn't know whom he should back, Asquith or Lloyd George, at this stage.

GLADYS. I see his predicament, but I'm more concerned about yours. Will anyone believe these words?

HESKETH. Yes, they will. I shall say I was there and copied everything into my journal that night.

GLADYS *looks incredulous and becomes sarcastic.*

GLADYS. Why on earth would the prime minister invite an out-of-work actor to dinner at 10 Downing Street, for God's sake? Will Ethel M. Dell be there as well?

HESKETH *becomes irritated and impatient.*

HESKETH. Of course *I* wasn't invited there. You haven't understood it at all. My name will not be on this book. It is an anonymous memoir written by an establishment figure.

GLADYS *is still incredulous.*

GLADYS. So what are you going to tell the fortunate publisher – if there is one?

HESKETH (*with a show of patience, as if explaining what is obvious*). I shall present myself as the author's friend. Say he insists on being anonymous and has asked me act as his literary agent. Simple.

GLADYS. And you really think it will sell?

HESKETH. I *know* it will. Let's listen to a bit more and see what we both think. Asquith has gone out of the dining room and Churchill is speaking directly to Lloyd George.

They switch on the recording machine again. HESKETH *resumes his acting and* GLADYS *shows her feelings, amused and worried.*

CHURCHILL. I wish you two wouldn't quarrel all the time.

HESKETH *and* GLADYS *look at each other and smile.*

LLOYD GEORGE. I *never* quarrel, Winston. You know that. But Asquith is getting impossible. He's letting the country go to the devil. If things go on like this I shall have to resign.

CHURCHILL My father used to say, 'Never resign until you're indispensable.'

LLOYD GEORGE. Rather a silly epigram, if you don't mind my saying so. But better than Asquith's platitudes.

CHURCHILL. The less said about politicians behind their backs the better.

LLOYD GEORGE. The trouble is that Asquith cannot look facts in the face. He thinks he knows everything because he went to Oxford. But I have nothing to say against him – and never will.

CHURCHILL *laughs.*

CHURCHILL. Would you like to take on his job?

There is the sound of a door opening and closing as ASQUITH *enters.*

CHURCHILL. What's the news, Prime Minister?

ASQUITH. I'm afraid there's been a setback on the Western Front.

LLOYD GEORGE. I told you so. If you don't do something soon, it'll be taken out of your hands, Prime Minister.

ASQUITH. In which case I will leave Downing Street and—

CHURCHILL. Really, I do think—

LLOYD GEORGE. Quiet, Winston! The prime minister is about to say something important.

ASQUITH. Yes, I was saying ... Would you circulate the port please, Winston ... I was saying ... What was I saying?

HESKETH's *laughter sounds on the recording and in the room.*

GLADYS *shakes her head.*

GLADYS. Well, I can see that *you* enjoy it. But will other people? Will they be taken in? What worries me is that we may be accused of libel or fraud or something.

HESKETH. It's a caricature, Glad – and there's no law against that. We're proud of our freedom of speech and I'm merely using that freedom.

GLADYS. The one thing I can see is there's no stopping you. So I'll not try any more.

HESKETH *goes over to* GLADYS *and hugs her. He is excited and goes back to his recording machine.*

HESKETH. Did I tell you I've invented my meetings with Lenin and Mussolini? It's becoming a tremendous rogues' gallery. And there'll be some royalty of course: George V and Edward VII. Then I'll add a misleading preface and the book will be complete!

HESKETH *sits at the desk and writes while* GLADYS, *with a gesture of despair, leaves the room.*

SCENE TWO

Three months later. A boardroom with bookshelves at the Bodley Head publishing house. DIANA *Pollen is sitting opposite* ALLEN *Lane. On a desk lies* HESKETH's *typescript.* DIANA *is pointing at the typescript and shrugging her shoulders in some bewilderment.*

DIANA. Apparently he simply came through the door with it. Said he was representing the author and then he walked out.

ALLEN *shakes his head in disappointment.*

ALLEN. I wish I'd seen him. I picked it up out of curiosity and couldn't put it down.

DIANA *smiles at him.*

DIANA. I haven't seen you so enthusiastic for a long time, Allen.

ALLEN *puts his hand on the typescript and speaks with great enthusiasm.*

ALLEN. It's one of the most exciting books I've ever read. The revelations are quite extraordinary – that's what gives it authenticity. We must bring it out this autumn and make it our lead title. You'll love it, Diana. There's hardly any editing to do.

DIANA. But who *is* the author?

ALLEN. I honestly don't know. Did you read the covering letter?

DIANA. You whisked it away before I had a chance.

ALLEN. The writer insists his book has to be published anonymously. But whoever he is, I cannot tell you. What I can say is it's our moral duty to publish it. Every page has the ring of truth. It'll be a bestseller, I promise you.

DIANA *looks at* ALLEN *closely and speaks with a degree of irony.*

DIANA. But do we at least know who brought us this mysterious masterpiece?

ALLEN *replies happily, smiling at* DIANA *and fumbling through some papers on the table.*

ALLEN. Yes, we do know. Here it is. His name is Hesketh Pearson. He's published some short stories and essays – and contributed political pieces to *The Times*. He strikes me as a straightforward sort of man. He's a friend of the author and has agreed to act on his behalf.

DIANA. Hesketh Pearson. Isn't he an actor?

ALLEN *is rather disconcerted.*

ALLEN. I believe so. But really Diana, you shouldn't hold that against him. We are in good hands, I can assure you.

DIANA *is gradually becoming dubious.*

DIANA. I remember. I saw him in a play called *The Fake*. He was rather good. But do you really think we can trust him? It's a most unusual arrangement. Surely we should find out more.

ALLEN *is put out by* DIANA's *reaction. He fingers his papers and clears his throat before reading rather pompously. He gets to his feet and walks round the table as he reads aloud.*

ALLEN. We do know more. Let me read you a couple of lines from the preface. 'Among the diplomats of Europe my name is a household word ... During the last thirty years my work has put me in close touch with most of the prominent men in Europe. I have met them in circumstances of privacy, when in fact they were most themselves...'

ALLEN *puts down the pages with considerable satisfaction.*

ALLEN. That should satisfy you.

DIANA *appears far from satisfied.*

DIANA. That's all very well, but it doesn't really help us. How do we know this actor isn't giving us another fake performance?

ALLEN *is becoming more persistent and impatient.*

ALLEN. You've been reading too much fiction, Diana. Let me read you a little more *non*-fiction for a change – from the preface again. 'I am amazed by the lack of first-hand portraiture of national figures in the memoirs we are given to read. In *my* book you will see these men faithfully drawn for the first time. The entire book has been compiled from a diary which I have kept since I reached the age of twenty-one.'

DIANA. Have you seen the diary, Allen?

ALLEN. I don't need to. How else could this have been written? It's obviously a diary.

DIANA *is becoming more obstinate.*

DIANA. But perhaps there is no diary – only Pearson himself.

ALLEN *is exasperated.*

ALLEN. Of course it's not Pearson! He would *never* have had access to royal families and prime ministers. Anyway, if we were shown the diaries we would know the writer's name – which he forbids. He doesn't want to be in the limelight and he can't break his code of secrecy. That's why he calls his book *The Whispering Gallery.*

DIANA. But what does it mean?

ALLEN *begins to feel more confident as he consults the manuscript. He clears his throat and prepares to read aloud.*

ALLEN. 'To move in high social circles you must live in a whispering gallery.' That's what he means. He explains it somewhere … Here we are. He writes: 'If my record remains a whispering gallery, it is chiefly so because some of the disclosures should be spoken only in a whisper as they travel down the long corridor of Time.'

ALLEN *pauses and smiles at* DIANA. *There is a silent moment.*

ALLEN. Rather beautiful that, don't you think Diana? Real poetry – 'the long corridor of Time'. Most affecting.

DIANA *is unaffected.*

DIANA. It could lead us down a long corridor of troubles.

ALLEN *is getting angry and more critical of* DIANA.

ALLEN. You are far too pessimistic, Diana. You see danger everywhere. It's not your fault, of course, but we are becoming too traditional, too safe. We desperately need to be bolder and find something that will sell – and sell rapidly. This book has got the smell of a bestseller. It's highly controversial and it has literary merit.

DIANA *looks very irritated by this criticism.*

DIANA. I'm not playing safe and I'm certainly not a pessimist. What you can't see is that this new author you like so much is a coward…

ALLEN *looks astonished and angry.*

ALLEN. That's absolute nonsense! How can you say he's a coward? You don't know him and you haven't read his book.

DIANA *is gaining the initiative and becoming more assertive.*

DIANA. I say it because he remains invisible and out of reach. Ours will be the only name on the title page and we will be the only ones taking any risk. He hides away whispering anonymously and we put a loudspeaker to his whispers. If there is a legal complication we will be the ones standing in the dock. You say we have a moral duty to publish this book. I say there must be someone who accepts the moral duty of writing it.

ALLEN *is impressed by this speech, but is sticking to his guns.*

ALLEN. What else *can* we do? If we threaten to put the author's name on the jacket he'll go straight to another publisher. We'll be the cowards if we don't take it on. We can't afford to miss such an opportunity …

DIANA *replies with sudden irony.*

DIANA. ... What about the opportunity of going to jail for libel? I wouldn't mind missing that.

ALLEN. Really you *do* exaggerate! No members of the royal family will take us to court and I can't see politicians entering the battle either – it will only give them more bad publicity and increase our sales. Some of the people in the book are dead and *can't* be libelled. The late Lord Northcliffe may turn in his grave as many times as he likes, but he can't hurt us.

DIANA. That's true. But Northcliffe's brother Lord Rothermere is very much alive. And his paper, the *Daily Mail, certainly* won't welcome us.

ALLEN *responds happily with some typical publisher-talk.*

ALLEN. That may be true. But bad reviews, I mean *atrociously* bad ones, will get us lots of attention. They sometimes sell as many copies as really good reviews, you know.

DIANA *is eager to change the subject and suggest a solution.*

DIANA. It's the legal aspect that really worries me. The least we can do is to get a lawyer's report before we go ahead, don't you think?

ALLEN *continues with his publisher-talk.*

ALLEN. No, I most certainly don't think so. It wouldn't help us at all. Do you remember that volume of erotic letters to the captain of a ship from his mistress? We published it a couple of years ago.

DIANA. Yes, I remember it – unfortunately. Not one of our better books.

ALLEN. I had a lawyer read the proofs. All I got was a very long, very expensive opinion, which didn't help at all. It was a masterpiece of indecision – on the one hand this, on the other hand that. Lawyers protect themselves rather than their clients. I won't make that mistake again.

The two of them are circling the table with The Whispering Gallery *papers on it as they search for a solution to their problem.*

DIANA. You could try another lawyer.

ALLEN. Believe me, they're all the same.

DIANA. Are you sure?

ALLEN. Absolutely sure! You've been in the business long enough to know that.

DIANA. But we must do *something* to protect ourselves.

ALLEN. I can't think what it could be...

DIANA. I have an idea.

They both sit down at the table.

ALLEN. All right. Tell me...

DIANA *and* ALLEN *lean towards each other at the table and begin whispering so that they cannot be heard.*

SCENE THREE

HESKETH *and* GLADYS's *apartment ten days later.* GLADYS *is tidying up the recording machine.* HESKETH *rushes into the room, very excited.*

HESKETH. Gladys! Gladys!

GLADYS. I'm here. What's wrong?

HESKETH. Nothing's wrong. Why do you always think something's wrong?

GLADYS. Because it usually is.

HESKETH *looks surprised.*

HESKETH. That's not true.

GLADYS *is amused.*

GLADYS. Yes it is. You are an excitable optimist and I am the realist.

HESKETH *smiles happily.*

HESKETH. That's why we get along so well. But I really do have good news for you.

GLADYS. I'll be the judge of that. Tell me what's happened.

HESKETH. I've just seen the managing chairman of the Bodley Head, Allen Lane.

GLADYS *seems worried.*

GLADYS. Why did you go there without telling me?

HESKETH. I didn't want to bother you.

GLADYS. I'm more bothered now. What happened?

HESKETH. What happened is that he gave me a contract for my book.

GLADYS. Go on.

HESKETH. I've got an advance of £250. He says *The Whispering Gallery* will be a bestseller.

GLADYS. Did you tell him what I asked you to do – tell him you were the author and made it all up?

HESKETH *looks a little shy and awkward.*

HESKETH. Not exactly.

GLADYS *is on the warpath.*

GLADYS. But you told me the publisher had written and explained that they needed to know the author's name before they could bring the book out.

HESKETH *is in retreat.*

HESKETH. Not exactly.

GLADYS *is becoming impatient.*

GLADYS. Stop saying that and let me know *exactly* what happened.

HESKETH. It's quite simple really. The publishers don't have to know the author's name – only Allen Lane has to know. Now do you understand?

GLADYS *looks completely bewildered.*

GLADYS. No, I don't understand. It makes no sense at all.

HESKETH. It makes perfect sense to me – at least it did when I was in their office.

GLADYS. Allen Lane *is* your publisher. If he knows who wrote the book, everyone else there will know – know it's you.

HESKETH *looks uncomfortable.*

HESKETH. Not exactly.

GLADYS. If you go on saying that, I'll walk out of this flat and leave you. I *must* know the truth. Tell me precisely who knows you wrote *The Whispering Gallery*.

HESKETH. Only we know. You and I, Glad. No one else, I promise.

GLADYS. But that's impossible. It makes no sense and it doesn't sound like good news at all to me.

HESKETH. It is a bit complicated.

GLADYS. You said it was simple.

HESKETH. It is simple – in a rather complicated way. Allen Lane is the only person who *has* to know and he promised to tell no one else inside or outside the building.

GLADYS. So you told him you were the author.

HESKETH *looks uneasy.*

HESKETH. Not exac— I told him someone else was.

GLADYS *gives a gesture of despair.*

GLADYS. You told him someone else was! Who, for God's sake?

HESKETH. I told him the author's name was Sir James Rennell Rodd.

GLADYS *looks incredulous.*

GLADYS. You're joking!

HESKETH. I promise you I'm not. The author of my book is now Sir James Rennell Rodd.

GLADYS. I've heard that name somewhere. Does he have something to do with toothpaste?

HESKETH *laughs.*

HESKETH. Toothpaste! He'd hate to hear you say that. He was our ambassador in Italy and our delegate at the League of Nations. In short, he's an establishment figure. He began as a poet and was encouraged by Oscar Wilde. But when Wilde went to prison he took against him. That's the sort of man he was – a turncoat – and turning his coat now.

GLADYS. Well, at least he's dead. That's something.

A look of awkwardness spreads over HESKETH's *face.*

HESKETH. Not exactly.

GLADYS *is exasperated.*

GLADYS. I *hate* that phrase of yours! What do you mean? Either he's dead or he's alive. Which is it?

HESKETH. He's retired – but is about to enter a new life in politics. He's in his seventies and a Conservative. Just the right age for a new Tory MP, don't you think?

GLADYS. This isn't funny, Hesketh. I can't believe you've been so foolish. Why didn't you simply say you were the author?

HESKETH. Because that would have seemed to make *The Whispering Gallery* a work of pure invention. I chose Rodd because he represents everything I dislike. I looked through his memoirs the other day in the library – all three volumes of them. A more pompous, self-important piece of political history I've seldom come across. It covers the same period as *The Whispering Gallery* and I have given him my book as a present.

GLADYS *interrupts him, hardly able to believe what she is hearing.*

GLADYS. This Rodd man – that's the name you really gave Allen Lane?

HESKETH. It is. Allen Lane must know Rodd could never have written such a book. He's no fool. 'That's our secret,' he said. We laughed, shook hands and he's added a clause to the contract stating that he will not disclose the name of the author. So we're safe – which is what you wanted.

GLADYS *puts her head in her hands.*

GLADYS. I think this book has sent you mad.

HESKETH *looks meek.*

HESKETH. I could plead insanity.

GLADYS. You may have to – and I'll visit you in a mental hospital instead of a prison.

HESKETH. I know you're worried. But I've been careful. There's no pornography or plagiarism. It's an entertainment, for heavens' sake, a comedy.

GLADYS. What you don't realise is that there's nothing people hate more than being laughed at. People without a sense of humour (and there are plenty of them) will take you very seriously. You've made them look like clowns. Your hero, Shakespeare, would know what I mean. You've read his words to me about 'that idiot laughter … a passion hateful to my purposes'. Hatred may be your reward too.

HESKETH *cheers up at the name Shakespeare.*

HESKETH. It's one of my favourite passages from the third act of *King John* where—

GLADYS interrupts him assertively.

GLADYS. You know where it appears – I know what it means. I really don't know how to get you out of this mess. Is it too late to withdraw the book?

HESKETH *is hurt by what she says about Shakespeare.*

HESKETH. It's far too late. They've already printed most of it. As for Shakespeare, he meant—

GLADYS. Forget Shakespeare! He's no use to you. There's only one thing you can do now. Have they given you the advance?

HESKETH *brightens up at the word 'advance' and searches for the cheque in his pocket and waves it in the air.*

HESKETH. Yes, they have. Here's the cheque. I told you there was good news. It's the largest cheque I've ever had.

GLADYS. Give it back. Give it back at once. Say we don't need it – say anything: but give it back.

HESKETH *is appalled and bemused.*

HESKETH. Are you serious?

GLADYS. Yes, I am very serious. You must not cash it.

HESKETH. But this money will change our lives.

GLADYS. Change it for the worse if we don't look out. If the book sells as you say it will, the money will come in due course.

HESKETH. I've always trusted your instinct, Gladys. It'll be painful, but I'll pop the cheque in the post tomorrow.

GLADYS. No, you won't. You'll go back and hand it back now.

HESKETH *reluctantly moves to the door.*

HESKETH. You're not usually so dictatorial. It was dictators who hated laughter. That's what Shakespeare meant.

GLADYS. Go at once, please.

HESKETH. I'm going. I'm going.

HESKETH *opens the door and leaves the room.* GLADYS *stands holding her head in her hands again.*

SCENE FOUR

Boardroom at the Bodley Head three weeks later. The table has on it a pile of books and newspapers. DIANA *is sitting at the table.* ALLEN *stands holding up a copy of* The Whispering Gallery *triumphantly.*

ALLEN. I told you it would be a bestseller, Diana.

DIANA *looks up at him, but is still worried.*

DIANA. But what about the reviews? Have you read them, Allen?

ALLEN *appears rather casual and amused.*

ALLEN. Some of them.

DIANA *goes through the newspapers and picks one out.*

DIANA. Did you see the *Observer*? 'Ghouls and Garbage' is the headline. It calls the author 'an imposter and a cad' and the book 'a reeking compost of falsehood'. I warned you of that sort of thing – and there's worse.

ALLEN. Yes, you did warn me. And I told you that bad reviews can sometimes sell as many copies as good ones. That is what's happened. It was the lead review, wasn't it, in the *Observer*?

DIANA. Yes, it was. But I don't think you know what's going on.

ALLEN. In what way?

DIANA *looks serious.*

DIANA. The book has moved from the review pages to the news pages.

ALLEN. That's excellent. I hoped something like that would happen.

DIANA *speaks with mounting anger.*

DIANA. It can't be good for our reputation. There has been a mass of complaints. We are accused of slandering the dead and impugning the integrity of British statesmen who helped to win the war. Some of the popular papers say the book is grossly unpatriotic. Need I go on?

ALLEN *looks rather disturbed.*

ALLEN. That's absurd. The attacks I've seen are trivial – misspellings and so forth. You mustn't get so worked up.

DIANA. I'm not worked up. This isn't trivial. We produced the book too quickly. People will think it's *my* fault as editor – but you took it from my hands.

ALLEN *speaks more gently.*

ALLEN. I'll make sure you have enough time to do the corrections before the next printing. We might even call it a *revised* edition. That should help sales. Perhaps we might even lower the price.

DIANA *looks surprised.*

DIANA. Why would you want to do that?

ALLEN. Because it would lead to a new market, a paperback market. That's an ambition of mine.

DIANA. It's a nice idea, I suppose.

ALLEN *takes up a page from the table to read.*

ALLEN. By the way, I sent out a press release last night. Here it is. 'We can vouch for the authenticity of this volume as we know the diarist personally. We believe the book to be perfectly genuine and there is no question of it being withdrawn.'

DIANA *looks at* ALLEN *in despair.*

DIANA. I don't think you were wise to make such a claim. You don't know the diarist personally – and nor do I.

ALLEN *looks at her with surprise.*

ALLEN. Why do you say that?

DIANA. Because it's true. You may have incriminated yourself – incriminated all of us. You haven't seen this morning's newspapers, have you?

ALLEN. No. Not yet.

DIANA *rustles through some of the papers on the table.*

DIANA. I should warn you – there are some very aggressive headlines. 'Scandalous Fake Exposed' … 'Insidious Bolshevist Propaganda'. That's ridiculous, of course. But the fact is *we* are being blamed as savagely as the author. Has anyone told you about Lord Birkenhead?

ALLEN. What do you mean?

ALLEN *seems at a loss. He comes to the table and stares at the pile of papers.*

DIANA. Someone suggested Lord Birkenhead was the author – and he's furious. He wants us to be taken to court. That will be the only way, he says, of stopping publishers making money from such falsehood. And he's a lawyer, remember.

ALLEN *is shocked.*

ALLEN. It does seem to be getting rather out of hand. Perhaps I should send out another press release.

DIANA *looks alarmed.*

DIANA. Please don't do that! We must come up with something quite new.

ALLEN. Such as what? We can't cave in. That would look like an admission of guilt.

DIANA. We must outmanoeuvre the enemy – I mean our arch-enemy, the *Daily Mail.*

ALLEN *seems disinclined.*

ALLEN. I don't see the *Mail* as our enemy. It has often helped us.

DIANA *holds up a copy of the* Daily Mail.

DIANA. Not any more. They call us 'A Disreputable Publisher'
– that's the headline. They say that the Bodley Head directors
'have uttered not a word of regret, not a word of apology, for
this outrage—'

ALLEN *interrupts her.*

ALLEN. That's incomprehensible. What can they mean?

DIANA. There's worse to come. I'll read it. 'The Bodley Head
have lent themselves to a fraud on the public and debased the
name of the firm. The *Daily Mail* has given orders that any
advertisement placed by the Bodley Head will in future be
rejected. Is there no law by which the publishers can be crimi-
nally prosecuted?'

ALLEN *is badly rattled by this.*

ALLEN. No advertisements – that's dreadful! Everything is
getting out of hand. We cannot afford to make an enemy of the
Mail – it's the most popular paper in the country. But how do
we get out of this mess?

DIANA. I have an idea. But you may not like it.

ALLEN *looks nervous and takes a deep breath.*

ALLEN. Shoot away.

DIANA. You should give the *Mail* another enemy to attack. First
of all you should speak to Sir Rennell Rodd himself and—

ALLEN *is greatly agitated by this suggestion.*

ALLEN. You mustn't mention his name, Diana. You're not
meant to know it, remember.

DIANA *impatiently brushes this aside.*

DIANA. We've passed that stage long ago. You must get hold of
Rodd and ask him straight out if he wrote the book. If he is the
author, he must make this known to the public. If he won't, we

will – you can put out another of your press releases making his authorship clear. Then we put the book out of print.

ALLEN *shakes his head, looking appalled at these words.*

ALLEN. That's unconditional surrender!

DIANA's *gestures make her statement all the more resolute.*

DIANA. If you do nothing things will get worse. You must do something – in fact you are the only person who can. There's no other way to get us out of this mess. If Rodd isn't the author, God help us.

ALLEN *attempts to charm* DIANA *into taking responsibility.*

ALLEN. I don't think I am up to this. Don't you think it would come better from a woman? You could do it much better than I could. You have great charm, Diana. I'd support you all the way, of course.

DIANA *is very firm in her rejection.*

DIANA. No! It has to come from the managing director: from you, Allen. If I spoke to him it would reveal that you told me his name, which you promised in the contract not to do. You'd be in an even worse pickle.

ALLEN. What an awful business this is!

DIANA *is unrelenting.*

DIANA. After you've spoken to Rodd, you'll have to go straight to the *Mail* and then—

ALLEN. That is the last straw. I'm beginning to hate those papers. We all have to dance to their tunes – not only us publishers, but politicians, even the police. They're far too powerful. They'll be ruling the country soon.

DIANA. That may be so. But it doesn't alter the fact that you will have to speak to the *Mail* today.

ALLEN. I really can't.

DIANA. Yes, you can. Otherwise you'll find yourself in court – and that you certainly don't want.

ALLEN *is out of his depth and in dismay.*

ALLEN. I can't believe any of this is happening to me. It's a nightmare. What should I say to the *Mail*?

DIANA *speaks with an authority that has gained on her over this conversation.*

DIANA. If, as I suspect, Rodd is not the author, you will say that you have been grossly misled by a most ingenious confidence trick. Following considerable investigation you have found the truth and will be withdrawing the book from publication immediately – as the *Mail* demanded in its leader. You will denounce Hesketh Pearson as the culprit – and offer deep regrets and sincere apologies for any offence the book has caused. You know the sort of thing.

ALLEN. This is not going to be very pleasant.

DIANA. There's a bit more. The *Mail* has called for the villain to be brought to court and, providing it supports us as one of the victims of this crime and withdraws its ban on advertising, we will do everything to bring Pearson to court for obtaining money by false pretences. That should do the trick.

ALLEN. I promised not to reveal the author's identity. It's in the contract. Won't I be breaking the law by telling people?

DIANA. No, you won't. Not if Pearson lied to you. You had to come clean and reveal what you were told. No lawyer would hold you to such a lie in the circumstances. There is no other course open to you.

ALLEN. Shouldn't I have a word with Mr Pearson first? He seemed such a nice chap.

DIANA. I already rang him.

ALLEN. You rang him? What did he say?

DIANA. He didn't say anything. His wife answered and told me he was 'not available'. She said their flat is being besieged by journalists. I heard some of them in the background shouting and banging at the door. They'll be at *our* doors next.

ALLEN *shudders and surrenders unhappily.*

ALLEN. I suppose you're right. I'd better ring Sir Rennell Rodd.

DIANA *is triumphant.*

DIANA. I have his telephone number here.

DIANA *hands it to him.*

SCENE FIVE

The Pearsons' home three weeks later. It is evening. The curtains are drawn. There is a sound of journalists chanting outside, which gradually fades. HESKETH *is lying on a sofa.*

HESKETH. I hate all this bloody uproar. It's hell.

GLADYS *comes over and sits opposite* HESKETH.

GLADYS. It's better than being in one of His Majesty's prisons. If the prosecution had had its way you'd have been locked up until the trial. Remember that and you'll feel better.

HESKETH *sits up and looks at* GLADYS.

HESKETH. I know. And I *would* have been in prison but for Dane. It's lucky for me my sister married such a generous man.

GLADYS. That's fine – so long as you don't think you married the wrong woman.

HESKETH *leans towards her and smiles.*

HESKETH. I'd never think that. I'd be lost without you. I was appalled when they set bail at £1,000. I was horrified when I saw how the whole thing was paraded through the newspapers. The sheer venom of it! I felt as if I was being accused of murder. I don't know what I would have done without you, Glad, I truly don't.

GLADYS. You'd have come through fine.

HESKETH. No, I wouldn't. It was you who made me return that £250 cheque before I was arrested. Thank God I did it. You know they altered the charge.

GLADYS. I still find that rather confusing. What *is* the charge now?

HESKETH. It was 'obtaining money by false pretences' and now it is '*attempting* to obtain money by false pretences'. If they hadn't changed it, I was told, the trial would have been at the

Old Bailey rather than the London Assizes tomorrow – and I would be languishing in jail these last weeks. What a fool I've been! I've let you down terribly.

GLADYS *comes and sits next to him, putting an arm round him.*

GLADYS. Nonsense! Don't be such a pessimist. It doesn't suit you. You're an optimist. Dane has marshalled an amazing team for your defence. To be represented by the Attorney General is astonishing.

HESKETH. You're right. But having someone as famous as Sir Patrick Hastings to defend me has given the press even more to write about. My real worry is how I am ever going to pay Dane back. And to think I wrote that book to take us out of poverty!

GLADYS. Dane isn't the only one to support you. You have other good friends.

HESKETH *begins to cheer up.*

HESKETH. That's true. Did I tell you Ivor Novello came across and wished me good luck the other day, and so did Freddy Lonsdale – he also offered me some money?

GLADYS. There you are, then.

HESKETH. I got a funny letter this morning from Frank Harris. He writes that I should tell the jury that memoirs are a well-known form of fiction and say that he had told me so. That should make the jury laugh, he reckons.

GLADYS *removes her arm from his shoulders and looks disapproving.*

GLADYS. They may well laugh, but they are more likely to send you to jail. Frank Harris is the last person you need. He's known only as a writer of pornography these days – some people say he's worse than D. H. Lawrence! He'll do your case no good at all.

HESKETH *nods in agreement.*

HESKETH. I suppose you're right. Bernard Shaw has also written. He says the best plan would be for me to plead guilty and
let my barrister persuade the judge I am a fool but not a knave –
in other words, throw myself on the mercy of the court. What
do you think?

GLADYS *is surprised and in two minds.*

GLADYS. Does he say what the more lenient sentence might be?

HESKETH. No, he doesn't.

GLADYS. You're not going to plead guilty, are you?

HESKETH *gets up and walks round the room.*

HESKETH. I don't want to. I don't *feel* guilty – though I don't
mind admitting I've been foolish. But I want to say why I wrote
the book, what I was trying to do. I haven't told you that Dane
wants me to tell Patrick Hastings about my war record – and
use that as a sort of explanation.

GLADYS *looks surprised and worried.*

GLADYS. What do you mean?

HESKETH. He wants me to tell the court what happened to me
in the war. You know – how I nearly died at the Front, was
mentioned in dispatches and awarded the Military Cross, and
so on. Then my barrister can tell the jury I am a wounded hero
subject to moments when I see red and go mad. Something like
that.

GLADYS *is anxious and protective but smiling.*

GLADYS. Perhaps you'd be mad not to use that defence. No jury
would feel easy at sending a wounded war hero to jail. Of course
you are maddening sometimes! You get fearfully hot under the
collar when you hear someone being rude about Shakespeare.

HESKETH *cheers up at the thought of Shakespeare.*

HESKETH. I should hope so too! Shakespeare saved my life
in the hospital. I recited his comedies while I lay in bed. The

doctors thought I was crazy but admitted I made a remarkable recovery. It just shows what a dose of Shakespeare can do!

GLADYS. Unfortunately I can't see him coming to your rescue tomorrow.

HESKETH. You never know. But I'm not going to parade my Military Cross in court to get myself out of this nightmare. That would be the very opposite of bravery. I've no idea of what I'm going to say. According to the newspapers, I'm already guilty and deserve a heavy custodial sentence. I never thought England had such a vindictive streak. I thought we'd left all that sort of thing behind with the war. It's depressing.

GLADYS *comes close to* HESKETH *and speaks gently.*

GLADYS. I didn't tell you this because I thought it would upset you. I've had packets of poisonous letters – all anonymous of course, all full of anger. Maybe your legal team should know that. They might make something of it.

HESKETH *is shocked. He puts his arms round* GLADYS.

HESKETH. Oh Gladys, I'm so sorry. I've put you through hell.

GLADYS. I'm quite a strong person, you know – stronger than you think I am. I am more worried about you – and you are worried about me. But whatever happens, they will not get the better of us.

HESKETH *starts walking up and down as he speaks.*

HESKETH. You're right. They won't. What shocks me is how people enjoy feeling outraged. I've always known it, but it still shocks me. All they want to see is what they call 'the impudent forger' punished. Well, I'm *not* going to plead guilty. I'm damned if I will – and will probably be damned if I don't. I've been chased through the streets, imprisoned in my home and pilloried by the press. I've had enough of it.

GLADYS. You'll know what to say once you are in court. After all, you're an actor – and the lines will come to you. But now we must go to bed. Tomorrow is going to be a long day.

The telephone rings, startling them both.

HESKETH. Don't answer it, for God's sake! It's bound to be another journalist asking silly questions.

GLADYS *walks across the room and picks up the phone.* HESKETH *is appalled.*

GLADYS. Hello ... Yes, this is Mrs Pearson ... He's here. What do you want us to do? ... I think they've all gone now – I can't hear anything... Yes, I understand. Do you mean now? ... I hope nothing awful has happened ... There's a back entrance and we are number twenty-three on the second floor. We'll see you in a few minutes. I'll tell him.

GLADYS *puts down the phone and turns to* HESKETH, *who has been* watching *her anxiously.*

HESKETH. Who was that and what are you going to tell me? No more bad news, please!

GLADYS. That was Sir Patrick Hastings, your barrister. He's in a car outside and coming up to see us. I've no idea if he's bring-ing good or bad news – but he doesn't want any journalists to see him or hear what he has to say. He's coming in by the back door and will be here in a minute.

HESKETH *looks anxious.*

HESKETH. Didn't he give you any clue of what he has to tell us? Have there been any developments?

GLADYS. I simply don't know. I've told you everything he said. We must just wait and—

There is a knock at the door and GLADYS *goes to open it.*

PATRICK *Hastings walks in and shakes their hands. The three of them sit down centre stage with the light on them.*

PATRICK. I'm sorry to disturb you at this late hour. But I felt I must see you – and this was the only way I could do so without drawing everyone's attention to us meeting. How are you standing up to the newspaper blizzard, Mr Pearson?

HESKETH. I've had better times. I'm not sure I've had worse – even in the war.

GLADYS *interrupts enthusiastically*.

GLADYS. He's doing fine, Sir Patrick.

PATRICK. Good. I'm glad to hear it. I know you've had discussions with my junior counsel, who represented you at the Marlborough Street Police Court when renewing bail. But I wanted to have a talk with you myself. Have you seen Sir Rennell Rodd's statement, Mr Pearson?

HESKETH *looks surprised but unenthusiastic*.

HESKETH. He's made a statement? I didn't know that.

PATRICK *takes out a piece of writing paper from his case*.

PATRICK. I must warn you he is not polite. I'll read a couple of sentences. This is what he wrote: 'It appears to me that there should be some action taken for the protection of the public in this matter… Perhaps the unkindest cut of all is that the author of the memoirs is said to use such abominable English.' It goes on in the same manner for a couple of paragraphs.

HESKETH. My style is hardly accidental.

PATRICK. What do you mean?

HESKETH. Rodd's style is like a voluminous eiderdown. It suffocates you. He keeps his readers warmly tucked up and half asleep. Everything is comfortable and there is no energy in it. He conceals far more than he reveals. I want to do the very opposite of that, something blunter and more direct, something wide awake that shows in everyday language an underlying truth, sometimes an unattractive truth. Mine is not a beautiful style – especially when representing someone I don't respect.

PATRICK *looks a little worried.*

PATRICK. I see. The trouble is that ordinary readers – such as the jury tomorrow – may feel sorry for this elderly gentleman who is some thirty years older than you. But I see from his statement that he has not read your book. So if the prosecution tries to use it, I shall object – object strongly. However, I need to know a little more. Tell me what your motives were for writing *The Whispering Gallery.*

HESKETH. I intended to make some money – I don't deny that. I'm not ashamed of wanting to earn money. 'No man but a blockhead ever wrote, except for money.' Those are not my words, Sir Patrick, they are Dr Johnson's. So I am in good company. I have ambitions to be a biographer, chiefly writing about the people I like.

PATRICK. What sort of people?

HESKETH. I want to write a life of the botanist and physician Erasmus Darwin. He was the grandfather of Charles Darwin and is my three-times-great-grandfather. After that I'd like to write a biography of that witty clergyman, Sydney Smith, a hero of mine.

PATRICK. Is there anything else I should know before going into court? What else have you written?

HESKETH. For the last couple of years I've been writing pen portraits of well-known people for *John Bull* – the magazine. I witnessed first-hand how skilful politicians tried to manipulate the press. They have such a wonderfully high opinion of themselves. I got sick of it. What I've done is to parody such people. I think that must be obvious.

PATRICK. I'm not sure this greatly helps us. You say your first motive was to make some money from your book. And whatever Dr Johnson may have said, the prosecution will seize on this as a confession of guilt. You write in one chapter, I see, that the Prince of Wales is so embittered after falling in love with a woman he can't marry that he is speculating on what might happen if he actually does marry her. I can tell you that this may be presented in court as an unworthy piece of gossip about a highly unlikely state of affairs. In other words, you will be called unpatriotic and accused of stirring up trouble where none exists. Sir Henry Curtis Bennett, who is leading the prosecution, may well cross-examine you on such matters. Do you know him?

HESKETH. No. I do not have that pleasure.

PATRICK. I should warn you that he is a formidable opponent. He is something of an actor in court. Makes a great entrance sometimes – he may remind you of Falstaff.

HESKETH *answers with unthinking pleasure.*

HESKETH. My favourite character in Shakespeare!

PATRICK *speaks with some amusement.*

PATRICK. He won't be your favourite character tomorrow. He made his reputation cross-examining spies during the war and since then has specialised in criminal prosecutions. He is a man of much guile and he likes winning.

HESKETH. That sounds very grim. What should I do?

PATRICK. It depends. If you plead guilty there is a reasonable chance that I can persuade the judge to bind you over for a year or two and let you go free – though Curtis Bennett will argue that you should be sent to jail as a warning to others. If you plead not guilty and the jury finds you guilty you are very likely to be sent to prison for six months or possibly even a year. It isn't for me to tell you what to plead. That is up to you – and of course your wife, who will also be affected by the verdict. So you must decide between the two of you. It would be easier for me if you let me know now. Do you wish to continue with your not guilty plea or change it now to guilty?

HESKETH *and* GLADYS *look at each other.*

GLADYS. May I say something, Sir Patrick?

PATRICK. Yes, of course, Mrs Pearson.

GLADYS *speaks with sudden passion.*

GLADYS. Hesketh is guilty. He is guilty of one thing – and that is being the most innocent man I have ever met. I have been married to him for fifteen years and I know what I am talking about. It's his innocence that has got him into this mess. I don't know about the law, but I believe it would be morally wrong for him to swear under oath that he is guilty. He would have that guilt on his record for the rest of his life and that would be unjust. He's often opinionated, sometimes irritating, lazy, hard-working, very charming, conceited and modest. You can't imagine what I sometimes have to put up with! But I wouldn't change places with anyone. Had he been a guilty man seeking money by fraud, he would have chosen a dead diplomat as the supposed author of the book. This may not make your job any easier, Sir Patrick. But it's the truth.

HESKETH *is much moved by what he has heard and is almost in tears.*

HESKETH. I ... I don't know what to say... I ...

GLADYS *smiles at him.*

GLADYS. I've never heard you say that before.

PATRICK *turns with a smile to* HESKETH.

PATRICK. Your wife has spoken for you. We will enter a plea of not guilty – and fight them all the way.

PATRICK *gets up to leave, shakes hands with* GLADYS *and* HESKETH *and puts on his coat.*

PATRICK. You are a good actor, I'm told, Mr Pearson. You would be wise to be directed by your wife at tomorrow's performance.

PATRICK *goes out of the door.* HESKETH *and* GLADYS *embrace.*

SCENE SIX

The London Assizes the following morning. The actors are all assembled in court, talking among themselves. HENRY *Curtis Bennett makes an extravagant Falstaffian entry, which* PATRICK *points out to* HESKETH. *The lights brighten and they all go to their seats. A* VOICE *calls out.*

VOICE. Mr Allen Lane to the witness box, please.

Everyone sits down and ALLEN *makes his way to the witness box.* PATRICK *stands up to question him.*

PATRICK. The Bodley Head is a distinguished publishing house I believe, Mr Lane.

ALLEN *is rather nervous but is happy to answer this amiable question.*

ALLEN. Yes. It is one of the best, probably the very best publisher in Britain today.

PATRICK. And you are the managing director of this 'very best' publishing house. I imagine you are proud of the books you publish.

ALLEN. I am very proud. We publish some outstanding books. But I am *not* proud of the book that has brought us here today. It is a book of lies.

PATRICK *gestures to the audience, which takes the place of a jury.*

PATRICK. That will be for the jury to decide. Am I right in saying that you publish classics as well as contemporary works?

ALLEN. Yes we do. We are especially proud of our classics.

PATRICK. I'm pleased to hear that. I have a few examples of your classics with me here. We'll begin with *The Golden Ass* by Apuleius, a Roman writer of the second century. It is, I see, what the Bodley Head call 'a romance'. Are you familiar with this book, Mr Lane – I see it was translated from African Latin. Is that so?

ALLEN *looks uncertain and out of his depth.*

ALLEN. I believe that is so.

PATRICK *opens a book and seems to study it.*

PATRICK. Good. I'd like to refer you to Book Seven. I have it
    open here. It's the page on which a murdered boy's mother,
    mad with grief, enters the stable where the murderer is lying
    and beats him with an iron bar. It's a striking passage, as I'm
    sure you'll agree. I'd like you to read the two paragraphs I
    have marked in the Bodley Head edition. It is an unforgettable
    scene where she thrusts a burning brand between his buttocks
    and he manages to put it out with a massive and malodorous
    evacuation. Some of the jury may not be as familiar with the
    event as you are, Mr Lane. So please read it slowly and begin
    with the sentence 'I unleashed at close quarters a stream of
    excrement...' I've marked the passage in red.

ALLEN *takes the book that* PATRICK *offers him and buries his
    head in it silently. He speaks very softly.*

ALLEN. Yes, I see it.

There is silence on stage.

PATRICK. I would be grateful if you would begin reading,
    Mr Lane.

ALLEN *does not look up.*

ALLEN. I am reading it.

PATRICK *is persistent, but polite. He gestures again at the
    audience.*

PATRICK. I mean read it aloud for the benefit of the jury.

ALLEN *looks shocked.*

ALLEN. I can't do that. It's out of the question.

PATRICK. On the contrary it *is* my question. Please begin.

ALLEN. No, I can't. What you are asking is impossible.

PATRICK. I'm sorry to hear that. Is there something wrong with the Bodley Head translation?

ALLEN. No, of course not.

PATRICK. Then what is the trouble?

ALLEN *lowers his voice and looks anxiously at the audience.*

ALLEN. There are ladies in court.

PATRICK. There are indeed – and in the jury too. They will want to hear a reading from the classics you are so proud of – as will the men. Surely your classics aren't for men only, are they?

ALLEN *is beginning to look very unhappy.*

ALLEN. No, of course not.

PATRICK. I'm glad to hear it. There's nothing on the book jacket to suggest it is only for male readers or for aristocrats to read in their private libraries. Surely it's for everyone. Would you, for example, expect one of your servants to read it?

ALLEN *answers the question rather pathetically.*

ALLEN. I only have one servant.

There is a pause while ALLEN *and* PATRICK *look at each other, neither of them knowing which will speak.*

PATRICK. And…?

ALLEN. And what?

PATRICK. And would you please answer my question. Would you allow this singular servant to read this … this 'romance'? Would she enjoy it?

ALLEN *looks bewildered before he answers.*

ALLEN. She is a man.

PATRICK. Very well, then. Would *he* enjoy reading it?

ALLEN. I've no idea. I cannot make guesses at other people's tastes in literature.

PATRICK *gets out another copy of the book and considers it as he speaks.*

PATRICK. I thought that was your job as a publisher. Let me come to your rescue, Mr Lane. I'll choose a more obliging page. What about one of the scenes of bestiality? There are quite a few to choose from. I don't know if you have a favourite. What about Book Ten, beginning with 'Wondering how I could mount such a fragile lady with my four hulking legs' and ending with the words 'our sexual performance'? That should give the jury a taste of the Bodley Head classics, don't you think? Do please begin.

ALLEN. This is ridiculous. You know very well I can't read that in public.

PATRICK. I know nothing of the sort. You put such writings into the public domain. The public is represented here today by the jury – and yet you refuse to read any passages from these books.

ALLEN *begins to recover himself.*

ALLEN. Private reading and public readings are completely different experiences. I refuse point blank to read aloud such passages out of context in this court.

PATRICK *picks up another Bodley Head book.*

PATRICK. Perhaps Apuleius, being a devout pagan, was an awkward choice of writer for you to read after taking an oath in the witness box. Let us go back much further and choose some poetry – some poetry by Ovid, which was written for speaking aloud. That should make things easier – in fact, there should be no difficulty at all. I've chosen a couple of passages from the Bodley Head's edition of Ovid's *The Art of Love.* Would that suit you better?

ALLEN *speaks more decisively.*

ALLEN. No, it would not. These classics call for sophisticated reading. They enable us to understand human nature by studying the past. What they give us is an intimate conversation between past and present.

PATRICK. Are we insufficiently sophisticated here in this court? Are these books beyond the comprehension of the jury? Is that your belief?

ALLEN. It is more subtle than that. All I can say is that the best readers of these wonderful books are scholars, scholars who specialise in literature from previous centuries.

PATRICK. This is all very disappointing, Mr Lane. We could have benefited from an explanatory reading from you. But we will have to get on as best we may without your guidance. Since you refuse to read your own books, I will show them to the jury – together with Balzac's *Droll Stories*. The simplest thing perhaps would be to show some of the illustrations, the explicit illustrations, which the Bodley Head decided to include in these books. To respect Mr Lane's sensitivities, I ask the ladies in the jury to look away if they wish.

A screen is rolled down so that the audience can see the pictures.

PATRICK *guides them through several pictures.* ALLEN *looks away.*

PATRICK. This first picture comes from Ovid's *The Art of Love*. I think it is clear what is happening. But perhaps you would like to add a caption or some art criticism, Mr Lane?

ALLEN *is quite angry by now.*

ALLEN. No, I would not! This is not an art gallery.

PATRICK *makes a hopeless gesture.*

PATRICK. Very well then, we will move on to *The Golden Ass. (He pronounces 'Ass' as if it had an 'r' in it.)* Here are two illustrations for you to consider, members of the jury … Perhaps that is sufficient for you – unless you would like me to show them something from Balzac's short stories, Mr Lane?

ALLEN *speaks very strongly.*

ALLEN. Putting such books before the jury in this style is entirely inappropriate, as you very well know. And let me point out that they have nothing to do with Hesketh Pearson's book – which is the reason we are all here.

PATRICK. I agree. Mr Pearson's book seems very innocent when compared to your classics – if that's what you mean.

ALLEN. That is *not* what I mean. You cannot compare these books with Pearson's stuff. And you can learn nothing of his dubious motives by referring to great classics from the past. You are misleading us.

PATRICK. In what way, may I ask?

ALLEN. In this way. Our classics are mostly works of fiction set in the distant past. They show us the culture of those times and we should read them in that spirit. From such imaginative works we can learn a good deal about human nature and our evolution. Pearson's work, on the other hand, purports to be a picture of contemporary life involving living people. But it is inauthentic, a work of invention, not of imagination. It is full of falsehoods. Every page has the ring of an untruth. It is a dishonest book, a confidence trick that can only mislead readers.

PATRICK. It's a pity you never spotted all these defects when you first read it. I daresay you would have preferred me to compare Pearson's book with some of your other contemporary publications.

ALLEN, *not realising he is walking into a trap, immediately agrees.*

ALLEN. Yes, that would have been more appropriate, certainly.

PATRICK. I shall follow your advice. I can see one recent Bodley Head publication that is very appropriate. The one I have in mind has no named author. It is anonymous – as Mr Pearson, you will remember, wished his own book to be. The book purports to be the letters from a lady to the captain of a ship. Do you remember it?

ALLEN *looks confused.*

ALLEN. I'm not sure I do.

PATRICK *picks up the book and shows it to* ALLEN.

PATRICK. Then let me remind you. I challenge you to read one single page of this Bodley Head book. I will be surprised if you find one that is not filthy.

ALLEN. But I am sure the anonymous author didn't pretend to be a knight of the realm, as Pearson did.

PATRICK. That indeed would have been difficult. It would have involved a miraculous change of gender which, I suspect, even you, Mr Lane, would have noticed. But who can say? A glance at Sir Rennell Rodd's entry in *Who's Who* would have told you that he could not possibly have been the author of *The Whispering Gallery.* Did you take any trouble at all to find out something about the person you apparently believed was your new author? Did you glance at the substantial volumes of his autobiography and see who had published them? Did you do anything except hurry the typescript into print so that you could make money out of it as soon as possible?

ALLEN. You don't understand anything about publishing. Besides, I trusted Pearson and found out too late that he was untrustworthy. That is the beginning and the end of the story.

PATRICK. Not quite, I think. Mr Pearson certainly trusted *you.* He brought you an anonymous memoir, which you read, liked and accepted. Later on you insisted on knowing the name of the author and promised to keep it a secret – you even added a secrecy clause to the contract. But as soon as there were questions asked in the newspapers, you broke the contract and told the world. You brought this trouble on yourself, don't you agree?

ALLEN. No, I do not. May I remind you, Sir Patrick, that it is Pearson who is on trial today? Not me.

PATRICK. And may I remind you, Mr Lane, that the Bodley Head is the only party that has made a profit from this book. I rest my case.

The cross-examination ends, the lights fade as ALLEN *returns to his seat and* PATRICK *sits down.* HESKETH *goes into the witness box. The lights brighten and* HENRY *Curtis Bennett, a man of great presence, stands up and begins his cross-examination.*

HENRY. You are an actor as well as a writer, are you not, Mr Pearson?

HESKETH. I am.

HENRY. All we really know about you is that you claim to be not guilty. It will need more time for the jury to know you better. You were in a play by Frederick Lonsdale recently, I'm told. Can you remind me of its name?

HESKETH. It was called *The Fake.*

HENRY. How very appropriate! You were obviously well cast. And is your book a fake too?

HESKETH. It is an entertainment.

HENRY. Unfortunately this is not a place of entertainment. It is a court of justice, Mr Pearson.

HESKETH *appears to be enjoying himself.*

HESKETH. I am grateful for your reminder. But I did not write my book here.

HENRY *becomes more aggressive.*

HENRY. But it has brought you here, your book. And it cannot have been a very entertaining journey for Sir Rennell Rodd, could it?

HESKETH. Is he here? He has not read my book and was unaware of it, I understand, until he was told about it by my publisher – against my wishes and against what had been agreed in my contract.

HENRY. So you are blaming your publisher for everything?

HESKETH. No, I am not. The Bodley Head is a leading publisher with a particularly fine range of classics as well as contemporary works, as you have heard.

There is some amusement and laughter among the actors in court. HENRY *is rather irritated by* HESKETH's *sally.*

HENRY. Very funny, Mr Pearson. You appear to be treating this matter very lightly. I must remind you that you are not playing in a West End farce but facing a serious criminal charge.

HESKETH *replies with some passion.*

HESKETH. I am very well aware of that. I have been chased through the streets by journalists, arrested by the police and am threatened with bankruptcy. I am utterly crushed by what seems like an avalanche that has descended on me. I can assure you that all this is far from being a comedy.

HENRY. It has indeed been a most destructive book, your *Whispering Gallery*. Everyone involved with it seems to have been damaged. Perhaps you would enlighten us and explain why you pretended, and went on pretending, that this eminent diplomat was the author. It is a mystery to me and many others, I believe.

HESKETH. The answer is quite simple. I chose him because I could not think of anyone less likely to have written the book. I knew, or thought I knew, that no one would believe me – it was a sort of private code between writer and publisher. Since Rodd's name did not appear on the book or in advertisements, he could not be identified or offended. I thought my publisher understood this, but apparently he didn't. Come to think of it, I don't know what he did understand.

There is some amusement among the actors in court; HENRY *puts an end to the laughter.*

HENRY. That is hardly the usual understanding between a writer and his publisher – hardly believable, I suggest. In fact it wasn't a code. It was a lie. You lied to your publisher and kept on lying in the hope of misleading the reading public. Those are the facts, aren't they?

HESKETH, *rather anguished, looks at* HENRY *and then round the court.*

HESKETH. Those are some of the facts. But you must understand I was in a panic. I was being attacked day after day – not only in the press and on the wireless, there were also lots of vitriolic letters to me and to my wife. I can't easily explain how I felt or what I did under such a barrage. I simply kept on repeating myself as a form of defence, a shield. I suppose I was mad – and that madness has led me here. Frankly, I feel I'm in a madhouse now.

HENRY. I'm sure you do not wish to add contempt of court to your other serious charge, Mr Pearson. You are doing yourself no favours. You seem unaware how disgusted the general public felt at what you did.

HESKETH. On the contrary, I am acutely aware of their hostility. Usually we talk about some scandal for a few days and then forget it. But occasionally things go further. We go on punishing some scapegoat, some whipping boy, until our anger is appeased and our virtuous outrage goes back to sleep. There are plenty of examples, from Byron to Wilde. I may have been experiencing a minor case of such hysteria.

HENRY. Thank you for that history lesson, Mr Pearson. I see you have little respect for morality – I think we all know that by now. Unhappily the people you name, Lord Byron and Oscar Wilde, are unable to appear on your behalf. And nothing you have said changes the history of this wretched book of yours. It is disingenuous and dishonest, full of malice and mockery. I put it to you: it is a shameful publication, a total fake, a forgery.

HESKETH. I'm glad you were not my reviewer as well as my prosecutor – the two are sometimes rather similar. There are plenty of trivial inaccuracies in *The Whispering Gallery*. I freely admit it. The book was an experiment, a far-from-perfect experiment, but a genuine one. Since the war, biographies have been changing and I want to be part of that change. I believe it our job to speculate, to test, to explore, to use our imagination – as Lytton Strachey has done.

HENRY. I have not interrupted your soliloquies, because every statement you make adds a fresh admission of your guilt. You appear to believe that you are privileged to write whatever you wish about the living and the dead. It's all the same to you. You write anything that comes into your mind – and to hell with those on the receiving end. You invent things merely to please yourself, merely to make a good story. You should try fiction – indeed, that is what you have done. You admit to having left all common sense behind when you attributed this 'experiment', as you call it, to someone you have never met. The only logical explanation I can give is that you gambled, hoping to make money from your gambling. That's the truth, isn't it?

HESKETH. What I have said is what I believe to be the truth. Perhaps that's why it sounds so odd. I believe there's an underlying truth in my book. The inaccuracies have been blown up out of all measure. It is not for them that I have been charged with a criminal offence and it was certainly not in my mind to obtain money by false pretences. I do not think along those lines. I do not and I did not.

HESKETH *goes back to his seat.* HENRY *looks through some papers and advances with them to the centre stage to make his closing address to the audience representing the jury. The light focuses on him.*

HENRY. Ladies and gentlemen of the jury, I have been given an excellent witness today for the prosecution. It is, of course, Mr Pearson himself. He enjoys paradox and has embraced it with exceptional determination. I do not envy my colleague, counsel for the defence, who has had the misfortune to represent him.

Obtaining, or attempting to obtain, money by false pretences is no minor misdemeanour, let alone a harmless joke, as the defendant seems to imagine. The contract he signed at the Bodley Head shows that he was due £250 as an advance on royalties – and that sum would have been multiplied more than ten times after the reprints came out – over £3,000, eventually. The fact that he did not avail himself of this advance once he realised that a criminal offence hung over him in no way lessens his guilt. Nor do I think that you should be sympathetic to his claim that he now faces bankruptcy. This is a predicament he has brought down on himself. No one else wrote this book. No one else is to blame.

My colleague Sir Patrick Hastings submitted Mr Lane to a fierce cross-examination. But I must point out that it was calculated to divert your attention from Mr Pearson's book – and that is the only book with which we should be dealing. You may think that Mr Lane was unduly generous to Mr Pearson, unduly lenient. But generosity and leniency are not crimes in our society.

The point has been made that Mr Lane acted illegally by revealing the name of the man he had been told was the author of *The Whispering Gallery*. But this agreement depended upon honesty, on truth – and honesty and truth were not what Mr Pearson gave his publisher. It was the author who broke the contract, not Mr Lane, who had no reasonable option but to walk away from the secrecy clause. It was a fake clause. Everything connected with this book has been a fake. The publisher has had the courage to admit in public that he had been fooled. It has been a humiliating experience for him – and it is Mr Pearson who put him through it – as he has put so many other people who are named in this wretched volume. Unless we show the public that such free and easy ways are not acceptable, we will be deluged with these mendacious and grotesque publications – what the leading critic of the *Observer* called 'garbage'.

The defendant has claimed he was mad when he lied to his publisher. But he was certainly not legally insane. A period of rehabilitation in Pentonville Prison would surely bring him to his senses. It would also act as a cautionary lesson for anyone else who is tempted to 'experiment' so selfishly, so greedily, and with such irresponsibility with the moral foundations of our culture.

The light fades as HENRY *sits down.* PATRICK *takes his place at the front of the stage. The light brightens and focuses on* PATRICK *with some papers in his hands.*

PATRICK. There can be no doubt that Mr Allen Lane very much enjoyed reading *The Whispering Gallery.* He had high hopes of it becoming a bestseller and treated Mr Pearson as its talented author.

You have heard that the advance on royalties was to be paid exclusively to Mr Pearson – as were all the royalties thereafter. Why, you may wonder, was he prepared to pay Mr Pearson the very large amount of money to be earned by this book if he believed that Mr Pearson had not written it? It makes no sense. And why had Mr Lane asked the defendant to name someone else in secret as the author – and then enter that name retrospectively in the contract? It was, I suggest, done to create an alibi for the Bodley Head and a get-out-of-jail card for Mr Lane himself should something go seriously wrong with this controversial publication.

The really naive person involved in this devious arrangement was not Mr Lane, as he would have you believe, but Mr Pearson, who had no notion he was being led into a trap. As a result it is he, Mr Pearson, who has been made the villain and left to take the blame for everything. Yet he is the only person in court who is telling the truth. Mr Lane never believed that *The Whispering Gallery* had actually been the work of Sir James Rennell Rodd, the secret author named in the contract. If he had believed it, he would have at least glanced at Sir Rennell's recent three-volume autobiography, where there is no mention of Hesketh Pearson as a friend or relative. How on earth could he explain why none of the royalties were being paid to this secret author? There can only be one reasonable answer: because he knew that this addition to the contract was pure make-believe. A distinguished diplomat Sir James Rennell Rodd may well have been, but not a saint, not a charity, giving away so much money to a stranger. If anyone in this courtroom is guilty of obtaining money by false pretences, it is surely Mr Allen Lane.

You have been told that Mr Pearson enjoys paradox. But it is parody that is his forte. He does not mimic other writers; he gives an absurd subtext to their writings and their speeches. He has produced an enthusiastic parody of the pompous self-regard that fills so many memoirs and hagiographies of politicians these days. Such memoirs are designed to promote the politicians' careers. By contrast, Mr Pearson is an amateur. He has made no progress at all either financially or on the promotion of his career as a writer. If he deserves punishment for his mischievous enterprise, he has already served it on himself. He is quite obviously no criminal. That he has a sense of humour is no crime – even bad jokes are allowable in a democracy.

What we have here is a book that the reading public has greatly enjoyed. Within six weeks it was reprinted several times. And where are the royalties from all these sales? Not in Mr Pearson's pockets. They are nicely locked up with other profits in the coffers of the Bodley Head, a publisher that has its eyes on dubious volumes circulated for money. Mr Pearson, as you can see, is not a natural money-maker by trade or instinct. He is, as he himself might have written, dangerously innocent.

The light fades and is then focused on the actors, who form two small groups. PATRICK, GLADYS *and* HESKETH *are on the left;* HENRY, DIANA *and* ALLEN *on the right. The focus is first on the left.*

GLADYS. I thought your speech was brilliant, Sir Patrick.

PATRICK. It was really your husband who won the jury round, I think. He made them smile and they took to him as if he were a hero in a comedy.

HESKETH. I have never felt less heroic in my life. But I was surprised by your attack on the Bodley Head classics.

PATRICK. I was sent those books by a rival publisher. It seemed a pity not to use them.

HESKETH. Good God! What knaves they are!

PATRICK. I wanted to discredit the Bodley Head, of course. But when the prosecution didn't intervene, I began to fear I was making the jury feel sorry for poor Allen Lane – or is it rich Allen Lane?

GLADYS. I didn't feel sorry for him at all. But I'm glad to hear that the jury took to Hesketh.

HESKETH. I never like to hear legal and moral judgements on literature. If I'd been Allen Lane I would have reeled off some pornographic passages, so-called, from Shakespeare. No one would have dared attack him for that.

GLADYS. Not in your presence, they wouldn't.

GLADYS *and* HESKETH *laugh and* PATRICK *smiles at them. The lights fade on them and focus on the other group,* HENRY, ALLEN *and* DIANA.

DIANA. How do you think it went, Sir Henry?

HENRY. It is a most unusual case. I think Sir Patrick made a mistake by alienating you, Mr Lane. It can't have worked in his favour. That's why I let him go on.

ALLEN. It wasn't a pleasant experience. I wasn't expecting it. I did the best I could. But frankly, I hope I never have to go into a witness box again.

HENRY. You did very well. Your obvious embarrassment was perfectly understandable.

DIANA. How long do you think the jury will be out, Sir Henry?

HENRY. It's difficult to tell. It depends very much on their attitude to the cross-examinations. They may take some time to disentangle it all. But in any case, it must be clear to everyone in court that Mr Pearson is…

The lights fill the stage and there is a sound of doors opening and closing.

DIANA. The jury's coming back.

ALLEN. I suppose I had better wait for the verdict.

HENRY. We must take our seats.

The actors sit and a VOICE *addresses the audience.*

VOICE. Ladies and gentlemen of the jury, do you find the defendant guilty or not guilty?

The lights go off and the set is prepared for the final scene.

SCENE SEVEN

The Pearsons' apartment three months later, with the trumpet-shaped machine there. HESKETH *is speaking into the telephone as* GLADYS *enters the room.*

HESKETH. I've read it. I liked it and I'll do it. See you next week, then.

HESKETH *puts down the phone and turns to* GLADYS.

HESKETH. I've got some good news for you, Glad.

GLADYS *looks at* HESKETH *warily.*

GLADYS. I hope it really *is* good news this time. You've been in a terrible mood these last weeks.

HESKETH. I suppose I must have been. I'm sorry. I've been getting on your nerves. I didn't know what to do with myself. I'm just waiting all the time – and I don't know what I am waiting for.

GLADYS. You must look on the bright side – that's what you usually do.

HESKETH *goes up to* GLADYS *and embraces her.*

HESKETH. There wasn't a bright side. I don't know what I'd have done without you, Glad.

GLADYS. You could be in prison. Remember that. But you were *not* guilty and you are free.

HESKETH *begins to cheer up.*

HESKETH. Did I tell you that I met some of the jury in the pub? They said they thought my book was amusing. I didn't feel amusing. But they laughed.

GLADYS. I certainly didn't laugh.

HESKETH *puts his hand into his pocket and brings out a letter and waves it at a dubious-looking* GLADYS.

HESKETH. But something rather funny has happened. I've had this letter from the Bodley Head. It contains an enormous cheque! They're paying me the profits on all the copies sold, as well as from the American publication. It's *thousands* of pounds! Allen Lane writes that he wants nothing to do with tainted money.

GLADYS. Very good of him at last! You'll be able to pay Dane for all those legal costs.

HESKETH. I certainly will – and we can have a holiday too.

GLADYS *looks at* HESKETH *carefully and there is a moment of silence.*

GLADYS. So what's the bad news?

HESKETH. What do you mean?

GLADYS. You know what I mean. I can see it in your face.

HESKETH. And I'll let you hear it.

He plays with the trumpet-shaped machine – and a VOICE *fills the room.*

VOICE. Seventeen copies sold – eleven to free circulating libraries beyond the seas. The earth might be uninhabited.

GLADYS. What was that?

HESKETH. That was me. I said it. I'm not the only one.

GLADYS. But what does it mean?

HESKETH. It means that no publisher will touch my work now. As a writer I'm dead – I've committed suicide. None of them will come near me. They see me as a liability.

GLADYS *comes up and comforts him.*

GLADYS. That won't last for ever.

HESKETH. Maybe not. But I don't know what to do with myself. I thought I might make a play of it – mixing fact and fiction together as Shakespeare did in his history plays.

GLADYS *shakes her head.*

GLADYS. Not Shakespeare again. Please! If you do write a play you'll only remind people of how obstinate you are!

HESKETH. You're right, of course. Perhaps someone else can write the play later on.

GLADYS. That's better. I don't want to see you in court again.

HESKETH. You won't. I promise.

GLADYS. So what *are* you going to do?

HESKET I'll have to go back on the stage. I read the script of a new play last week and have been offered a leading role. It's going on tour in three or four months. I've just phoned them to say I'll do it. It's not so much a matter of the money. It's that I can't hang around here getting in your way and doing nothing. You know what I mean.

GLADYS *smiles at him.*

GLADYS. I certainly do. What's the play?

HESKETH. It's an American melodrama. I play the villain.

GLADYS. Sir Henry What's-His-Name – Curtis Bennett – will like that.

HESKETH. I'm not so sure he will. It's called *The Acquittal.*

HESKETH *and* GLADYS *embrace each other, laughing. The curtain comes down.*

End of play.

Programme Note

Allen Lane went on to found Penguin Paperbacks in 1935 and was later knighted for services to publishing. In 1960 he appeared in court successfully defending the Penguin unexpurgated edition of D. H. Lawrence's *Lady Chatterley's Lover*.

Hesketh Pearson's lives of Erasmus Darwin, Sydney Smith, Oscar Wilde and Shakespeare were among his biographies published by Penguin. He was elected in the 1940s as a Fellow of the Royal Society of Literature. In *Who's Who* he did not list *The Whispering Gallery* among his publications or put on record having been awarded the Military Cross during the First World War.

Sir James Rennell Rodd became a Conservative Member of Parliament and in 1933 was created a life peer as Baron Rennell of Rodd. One of his sons, Peter Rodd, married Nancy Mitford, who portrayed him as Christian Talbot in *The Pursuit of Love*. He also helped to inspire one of Evelyn Waugh's most notorious characters, Basil Seal.

Financial note: £250 pounds in 1926 would be worth more than £12,000 today.

A Note on the Author

Michael Holroyd is one of our leading biographers. He has written the definitive biographies of Lytton Strachey, Bernard Shaw and Augustus John, as well as a group biography of Ellen Terry, Henry Irving and their families. He was awarded a knighthood in 2007 for services to literature. He lives in London.

A Note on the Type

The text of this book is set in Linotype Stempel Garamond, a version of Garamond adapted and first used by the Stempel foundry in 1924. It is one of several versions of Garamond based on the designs of Claude Garamond. It is thought that Garamond based his font on Bembo, cut in 1495 by Francesco Griffo in collaboration with the Italian printer Aldus Manutius. Garamond types were first used in books printed in Paris around 1532. Many of the present-day versions of this type are based on the *Typi Academiae* of Jean Jannon cut in Sedan in 1615.

Claude Garamond was born in Paris in 1480. He learned how to cut type from his father and by the age of fifteen he was able to fashion steel punches the size of a pica with great precision. At the age of sixty he was commissioned by King Francis I to design a Greek alphabet, and for this he was given the honourable title of royal type founder. He died in 1561.